café food at home

Rosanna Thomson

café food at home

over 200 simple and easy to follow recipes

NEW
HOLLAND

introduction

A café is a little oasis away from the daily grind, where you can sit back and relax with a good meal and chat with family and friends. Cafés are social places where anyone can indulge in a three-course meal or simply stop in for a short coffee break. There are no hard and fast rules to enjoying the atmosphere in a café – just savour the experience and the coffee aroma. What sets café food apart from fine dining in fancy restaurants are the versatile recipes that are perfect for all ages and palates. There is bound to be a meal that will cater to your appetite at any time of the day. This immediately sets the tone for relaxed eating in a friendly environment.

As our lives get busier and more complicated, the popularity of café dining has risen because of its simplicity, affordability and varied flavours – most people even have a favourite haunt of their own. Whether it be for breakfast, lunch, a break for coffee and cake, dinner or a late-night snack, café food offers a range of menu options that can be easily imitated at home. With the abundance of fresh produce available and the help of this book, you can now create delicious café food in your own kitchen.

Café food at home is a collection of the classic dishes found in most cafés. With an emphasis on relaxed eating with meals that are quick and easy to prepare, you'll find recipes to suit any occasion. Most of the recipes are effortless, so that you are not stuck in the kitchen preparing complicated meals and missing out on entertaining your guests. All you have to do is work out a menu, use good seasonal produce, put your favourite music on, and enjoy the casual ambience cooking café food at home can bring.

beverages

afternoon kick

Serves 1

1 carrot, top and bottom removed and peeled | 1 Granny Smith apple, cored and quartered
1 orange, peeled, seeded and quartered | 2 teaspoons fresh ginger, roughly chopped

Juice carrot, orange and apple together. Transfer mix to a blender and process with ginger. Strain juice to remove ginger fibres and serve.

banana and mango frappé

Serves 1

1 ripe banana, peeled and chopped | 1 small mango, peeled and chopped
6 ice cubes |

In a blender, combine all ingredients and blend until smooth and frothy. Serve immediately.

berry smoothie

Serves 1

1 cup fresh berries | ½ cup (4 oz) natural yoghurt
(strawberries, raspberries, blueberries) | 1 cup (8 fl oz) milk
6 ice cubes | ½ tablespoon honey

Combine all ingredients in a blender until smooth and serve.

breakfast in a glass

Serves 2

1 cup (8 fl oz) milk
½ cup (4 oz) natural yoghurt
1 ripe banana, peeled and chopped
1 cup fresh strawberries

2 tablespoons almond meal (see glossary)
1 tablespoon sunflower seed meal (see glossary)
2 teaspoons wheatgerm (see glossary)

In a blender, combine all ingredients and process until smooth and frothy. Serve immediately.

coconut heaven

Serves 1

1 cup strawberries, hulled
1 banana, peeled and chopped

2 tablespoons coconut milk
4 ice cubes

Place strawberries, banana, coconut milk and ice in a blender and process until smooth and frothy. Serve chilled.

hot chocolate

Serves 4

3 tablespoons cocoa	½ cup (4 fl oz) water
2 tablespoons sugar	2½ cups (20 fl oz) milk
pinch of salt	4 marshmallows

Place cocoa, sugar, salt and water in a saucepan. Mix well. Bring to boil over a low heat. Boil gently for a few minutes, stirring all the time.

Add milk. Heat thoroughly, stirring continuously, but do not boil.

Beat with a hand beater until foamy.

Pour hot chocolate into four mugs, add a marshmallow to each one, and serve.

iced coffee

Serves 6

250 g (8 oz) medium ground coffee	1 L (32 fl oz) milk, chilled
pinch of salt	1 cup (8 fl oz) thick cream
3 cups (24 fl oz) freshly boiled water	6 scoops of vanilla ice-cream

Put coffee and salt into a large coffee plunger. Pour over boiling water. Allow to stand until cool, then plunge. Chill for a few hours.

Just before serving, mix chilled milk with coffee. Pour into tall glasses.

Whip cream until fairly stiff.

Place a scoop of ice-cream into each glass and top with whipped cream. Serve immediately.

iced tea

Serves 4

6 teaspoons tea leaves or 6 teabags | juice of 3 lemons
3 cups (24 fl oz) boiling water | ice cubes
½ cup (4 oz) sugar | mint sprigs, to garnish
3 cups (24 fl oz) cold water | lemon wedges, to garnish

Infuse tea with boiling water and add sugar. When cold add three cups cold water and lemon juice. Chill in the refrigerator. Serve over ice cubes and garnish with sprigs of mint and lemon wedges.

mocha fino

Serves 1

½ cup (1½ oz) double strength espresso | 1 teaspoon ground cinnamon
½ cup (4 fl oz) boiling water | ¼ cup (2 fl oz) milk
1 tablespoon sugar | extra cocoa, to garnish
1½ teaspoons cocoa |

Place coffee in a coffee plunger. Pour over boiling water. Allow to stand for two minutes then plunge.

Place sugar, cocoa and cinnamon in a large cup. Pour over espresso and stir. Steam milk in a cappuccino machine or froth by blending hot milk on high speed in a blender. Pour milk over coffee and serve with extra cocoa sprinkled on milk foam.

orange, pineapple and mango juice

Serves 1

1 large orange, peeled, seeded and chopped
1 mango, peeled and chopped

¼ pineapple, peeled, cored, and chopped

In a juicer, process orange, mango and pineapple. Serve immediately in a tall glass.

orange sunrise

Serves 1

1 orange, peeled, seeded and quartered
1 lemon, peeled, seeded and quartered

3 carrots, tops and bottoms removed and peeled

Juice orange and lemon in a juicer and set aside. Juice carrot, pour into orange and lemon mix and combine. Serve chilled.

pineapple and coconut juice

Serves 1

½ pineapple, peeled, cored and chopped
½ cup (4 fl oz) coconut milk

6 fresh mint leaves, finely chopped

In a juicer, process pineapple, then pour into a tall glass. Stir in coconut milk and mint. Serve.

rise and shine

Serves 1

2 oranges, peeled, seeded and quartered
1 banana, peeled and chopped

1 passionfruit, pulp scooped out

Juice oranges. Transfer orange juice to a blender, add banana, and blend until well combined. Pour juice into a tall glass and stir in passionfruit. Serve immediately.

strawberry smoothie

Serves 1

1 cup (8 oz) natural yoghurt
handful of crushed ice

1 handful strawberries
1 teaspoon honey

Combine all ingredients in a blender and process until smooth and creamy. Serve immediately.

Note: Strawberries can be substituted for other fruits, or a variety can be added, such as banana and mango.

wake-up call

Serves 1

2 pears, peeled, cored and quartered
1 apple, peeled, cored and quartered

8 prunes, pitted

Juice pears and apple together in a juicer. Transfer mix to a blender and add prunes. Blend until well combined and serve.

cinnamon lemongrass tea

Serves 4

3 long cinnamon quills | 1 small lemon, cut in halves
6 long pieces green lemongrass leaves | 1 L (32 fl oz) boiling water

Break the cinnamon quills in half and drop into a teapot with the lemon halves.

Crush the lemongrass leaves and add to the other ingredients. Top with boiling water and leave to steep or infuse for 10 minutes.

Strain and drink hot, warm or at room temperature.

This is really refreshing as a hot drink and is good chilled too. Strain it into a glass container before chilling. Don't keep much longer than a day as the aroma that makes it so attractive slowly dissipates when storing. You can pour it over ice with some lemon slices in summer for a long drink any time of day.

Cinnamon quills or sticks are the best to use.

italian style iced chocolate

Serves 1

4 large scoops chocolate ice-cream | 1 sachet or 2 teaspoons chocolate milk powder
1 cup (8 fl oz) full-cream milk |

Make up the chocolate milk by dissolving the milk powder in a small amount of hot water and adding the full cream milk. Pack a tall glass with the chocolate ice-cream and pour the chocolate milk over the ice cream.

chocolate, banana and kiwifruit smoothie

Serves 3

100 g (3½ oz) fat-free chocolate swirl ice-cream | 150 g very ripe bananas
1 kiwi fruit, peeled | 1 tablespoon lemon juice
2 cups (16 fl oz) skim milk | ½ teaspoon powdered cinnamon

Place all ingredients, except the cinnamon, in a blender and work until combined. Pour and sprinkle with cinnamon.

This is a great afternoon snack.

mango smoothie

Serves 2

1 fresh mango or one 275g (10 oz) tin of mango | 6 tablespoons Greek or thick yoghurt
1 cup full-cream milk | 1 teaspoon vanilla essence

Combine all ingredients in a blender for 1 minute and serve immediately. Add passionfruit for a different tang.

green tea

To serve sen-cha for 1

Choose a small teapot.
Pour boiled water into a tea cup. Transfer the water to the pot.
Pour the water back into the tea cup.
Put approximately 2 teaspoons of green tea leaves into the pot and pour over water from the tea cup.
Wait for one minute and serve.

When you make tea in a large teapot, use water between 70-80°C (160-180°F). This is the best temperature to brew the tea.

Genmai-cha is sen-cha green tea combined with roasted unpolished brown rice. It has an aromatic flavour and is quite a refreshing drink. The best temperature to brew it is about 95°C (200°F).

Hōi-cha is roasted green tea, which has less caffeine and less bitterness. You can use up stale green tea by roasting the leaves on baking paper in a frying pan over a low heat to make hoji-cha. The best temperature to brew it is about 95°C (200°F).

Maccha is powdered green tea. To brew, pour hot water into a tea bowl to warm. Using a chasen (bamboo whisk), moisten the bowl then discard the water. Wrap the bowl in a muslin cloth and using a chashaku (bamboo teaspoon), add about 2 grams of tea powder and pour about ¼ of a cup of hot water. Whisk with the chasen.

Japanese green tea is dried without fermentation. After picking the leaves, they are sterilised with steam or roasted. There are various varieties of green teas but sen-cha is the most popular and familiar. The best quality of sen-cha is called gyokuro, which is made only from young leaves covered and protected from the sun for twenty days which means it has less bitterness and a fuller flavour.

Green tea is very delicate; it easily loses quality by exposure to moisture, light and temperature extremes. So it is better to keep it in an airtight box and away from the direct light.

moroccan mint tea

Serves 4
(2 glasses each, traditionally it is 3 each but see how you go)

½ cup (4 oz) Chinese gunpowder (or green) tea
1 bunch spearmint (preferably a short, curly bunch with red stalks), washed

1 L (1½ pints) boiling hot water plus 1 extra cup for washing the pot
½ cup (4 oz) sugar

Place the tea into the pot and pour in the cup of boiling water, swish around then strain the water out leaving the leaves inside. This is the traditional way to clean the leaves and remove the bitterness.

Pour in the litre of boiling water and allow to boil for 1 minute over hot embers (or on the stove top).

Stuff the spearmint tightly into the pot and place back on the heat for a few more seconds.

Add in the sugar and allow to dissolve.

Using a tea towel to protect your hands, pour out a glass, then pour it back into the pot, repeat another two times, this allows the tea to properly mix and infuse. Try the tea first before serving to ensure it is well mixed.

Serve the tea into the other glasses, pour from high up and come down towards the end to create froth.

Be sure not to pour to the top, leave a rim of about 3 fingers deep for the person to hold the glass by. The person preparing the tea is the only person to pour until the pot is empty and each glass is to be handed to the right. These are the traditional guidelines for a mint tea 'ceremony', have fun with it and enjoy.

Serve in a large metal teapot.

arabic coffee

Serves 4

1½ cups (12 fl oz) water	4 teaspoons Turkish (or any finely ground) coffee
2 teaspoons raw sugar	3 cardamom pods, cracked
1 clove	1 cinnamon stick

In a small saucepan, bring the water to boiling point before turning off the heat.

Add in the coffee, sugar, cardamom, clove and cinnamon stick and bring back to the boil. Keep boiling until the froth starts to rise then turn off the heat.

When the froth starts to dissolve and has settled, stir, then turn the heat back up again, allowing to boil and the froth to rise again.

Serve the coffee straight away with an equal share of the froth in each glass.

Allow to cool and settle for a moment before drinking.

Serve with Moroccan biscuits.

Drinking Arabic coffee in Morocco is like drinking a pot of tea in Australia. Moroccans love to drink it sitting outside a café European style, whilst at home it's served as an occasional treat. Each household has its own blend, the spices vary. This recipe is for a sweet, spiced coffee with a perfume as strong as its flavour.

breakfast

blackberry muffins
with blackberry cream

Makes 12

2½ cups (6 oz) plain (all-purpose) flour
2 teaspoons baking powder (see glossary)
½ cup (4 oz) sugar
100 g (3 oz) butter
¼ cup (3 oz) golden syrup
2 eggs
2 teaspoons baking soda (see glossary)
1 cup (8 fl oz) skim milk
1½ cups (6 oz) fresh blackberries
or frozen blackberries, thawed
icing (confectioners') sugar

BLACKBERRY CREAM
2 tablespoons blackberry juice or blackberry purée (if using frozen blackberries, chances are you will get some juice when the berries thaw, otherwise mash a few blackberries to make the purée)
1 teaspoon icing (confectioners') sugar
½ cup (4 oz) light sour cream

Preheat oven to 190°C (375°F).

Sift flour and baking powder into a bowl. Stir in sugar, then make a well in the centre of the dry ingredients.

In a saucepan over low heat, melt butter and golden syrup.

In a separate bowl, lightly beat eggs.

In another bowl, dissolve baking soda in the milk.

Pour butter, eggs and milk mixtures into the dry ingredients. Add blackberries and mix gently to just moisten the ingredients. Three-quarters fill a greased 12-cup muffin tin with the mixture. Bake for 20 minutes or until muffins spring back when lightly touched.

Serve warm, dusted with icing sugar and accompanied by blackberry cream.

To make the blackberry cream, mix blackberry juice (or purée), icing sugar and sour cream together.

eggs benedict

Serves 1-2

	HOLLANDAISE SAUCE
2 slices of bread	2 egg yolks
butter or margarine, for spreading	pinch of cayenne pepper
2 eggs	salt and freshly ground black pepper, to taste
2 slices of ham	1-2 tablespoons lemon juice or
	white wine vinegar
	90 g (3 oz) butter

First, make the hollandaise sauce. Bring some water to the boil in the base of a double boiler. Put egg yolks, seasonings and lemon juice into the top of the double boiler. Whisk mixture over boiling water until sauce begins to thicken. Add butter, in very small pieces, whisking in each piece until completely melted before adding the next. Do not stop stirring and do not allow sauce to boil, or it will curdle. If the sauce is too thick, add a little cream.

Cut a large round from each slice of bread. Spread butter or margarine on both sides and fry until golden on both sides.

Next poach the eggs (see page 32).

Preheat grill. Cut ham to fit the fried bread, set on top of the bread and place on plates.

Top with poached eggs, then spoon over hollandaise sauce. Place under hot grill for about two minutes to brown lightly.

cinnamon toast

Serves 3

125 g (4 oz) caster (superfine) sugar	6 slices white bread
2-3 teaspoons ground cinnamon	butter, softened

Mix sugar and cinnamon in a bowl.

Toast the bread lightly on both sides and butter one side, spreading the butter right to the edges. Using a spoon, sprinkle each slice of toast evenly with the cinnamon and sugar mixture. Put the toast under the grill and cook until the sugar starts to melt. Remove and serve hot.

french toast

Serves 4

3-4 eggs	pinch of salt
½ cup (4 fl oz) milk	butter, for frying
2 tablespoons caster (superfine) sugar	8 thick slices of bread
¼ teaspoon of vanilla essence	

In a large bowl, combine eggs, milk, sugar, vanilla essence and salt.

Heat a little butter in a frying pan over medium heat. Dip a slice of bread into the egg mixture until bread is completely coated and has soaked up some egg mixture. Place bread in the frying pan and cook for one minute on each side or until it is crisp and golden. Repeat with remaining bread, until egg mixture has all been used.

Goes well with maple syrup, bacon and fried or raw banana.

porridge

Serves 2

1 cup (3 oz) rolled oats	pinch of salt (optional)
1 cup (8 fl oz) cold water	1½ cups (12 fl oz) near boiling water

Blend oats, cold water and salt in a saucepan. Add near-boiling water and stir vigorously. Boil for five minutes, stirring frequently until oatmeal mixture is thick and creamy.

Serve with a little honey, brown sugar or dried fruit.

full breakfast with fried eggs

Serves 1

1 rasher of bacon, rind removed	1 egg
1 breakfast sausage	1 tomato
1 large mushroom, sliced	

Place bacon, sausage and mushroom in a cold pan without fat and fry slowly until the bacon fat is clear, and the sausage has browned. Lift onto a hot dish and keep warm.

Wash and dry tomato, cut into thick slices or in half.

Heat leftover bacon fat in the frying pan, add tomato and cook for two minutes.

Break egg into a saucer and slide carefully into the pan alongside the tomato. Cook slowly, turning egg if desired. When set, lift egg out with a spatula followed by the tomato and place on a plate with the bacon, sausage and mushroom.

Serve with hot buttered toast.

potato patties

Serves 4

450 g (1 lb) potatoes, peeled and cut into even-sized chunks
good knob of butter or margarine
2 tablespoons plain (all-purpose) flour

salt and freshly ground black pepper to taste
1 egg, beaten
75 g (2½ oz) dried breadcrumbs
¼ cup (2 fl oz) olive oil, for shallow frying

Place potatoes in a large saucepan and cover with cold water. Add a good pinch of salt. Cover pan and cook over a high heat until water boils, then lower heat a little and continue to cook for 10–15 minutes (depending on their size) until potatoes are tender.

Drain potatoes in a colander, return them to the pan and mash them well with butter or margarine, using a fork or potato masher. Briskly stir in flour and salt and pepper using a wooden spoon.

Shape potato into small, flat patties, brush with beaten egg and roll in breadcrumbs. Chill until ready to cook.

Heat oil in a frying pan until hot, but not smoking, then turn down heat to medium and shallow-fry patties for about four minutes, turning occasionally, until golden brown. Drain on kitchen paper and serve hot.

pancakes with maple syrup

Makes 8

125 g (4 oz) self-raising (self-rising) flour
pinch of salt
½ teaspoon bicarbonate of soda (see glossary)
1 cup (8 fl oz) milk

3 tablespoons caster (superfine) sugar
1 egg
butter for frying
maple syrup

Preheat oven to 100°C (200°F).

Place flour, salt, bicarbonate of soda, milk, sugar and egg in a mixing bowl and beat until there are no lumps.

Melt a small piece of butter in a frying pan over medium heat. Ladle a little pancake mixture into the centre of the pan. The mixture should spread out to about 15 cm (6 in) across. Cook until the bubbles on top have burst, then flip the pancake over using a spatula. Cook for another about two minutes or until the underside is golden brown, then lift the pancake onto a plate. Repeat until all mixture is used.

As pancakes are cooked, stack them on a plate, cover with aluminium foil and put in the oven to keep warm. Serve with maple syrup.

Variation: Serve pancakes with lemon and sugar or fresh berries and cream instead of maple syrup.

poached eggs

Serves 2

| 4 eggs | pinch of salt |
| dash of white vinegar | salt |

Half-fill a deep frying pan with water and bring to the boil. Add vinegar (this prevents the whites from spreading) and salt.

Break each egg onto a saucer and slide it into the boiling water. Cook for about three minutes, or until whites are set.

Remove eggs with a slotted spoon, drain carefully, and serve on buttered toast.

Like all egg dishes, poached eggs must be served the moment they are cooked,
so toast and butter the bread while the eggs cook.

scrambled eggs

Serves 4

8 eggs	1 tablespoon fresh herbs, finely
salt and freshly ground black pepper, to taste	chopped (optional), and extra to garnish
1 tablespoon butter	

In a bowl, beat eggs very lightly with salt and pepper. Add herbs (if using). A small amount of herbs may be kept for a garnish.

Place butter in a frying pan and melt over a low heat. Pour in egg mixture and, using a broad wooden spatula, scramble egg slowly across pan as it thickens. When cooked to desired consistency, remove from heat. Turn onto a warm plate, sprinkle with extra herbs and serve at once with buttered toast.

Variation: Finely grated cheese can be sprinkled on top when serving.

spanish omelette

Serves 2

	FILLING
3 eggs	45 g (1½ oz) butter
salt and freshly ground black pepper, to taste	3 tablespoons green capsicum (bell pepper), seeds and pith removed, and thinly chopped
1 tablespoon water	3 tablespoons red capsicum (bell pepper), seeds and pith removed, and thinly chopped
1 tablespoon butter	1 onion, thinly chopped
	1 stalk celery, thinly chopped
	salt and freshly ground black pepper, to taste

In a bowl, very gently beat eggs, salt and pepper and water together. Set aside.

To make the filling, melt butter in a small saucepan, add vegetables, salt and pepper, and cook slowly without browning. Keep hot.

Heat butter in a large frying pan, and when gently bubbling, transfer the cooked filling to this pan. Shake it to level over the base, then pour egg mixture on top. Shake the pan gently as the eggs cook. When the omelette is set, loosen the edges and run a palette knife underneath.

Slide the omelette to the edge of the pan (without folding) and turn it over, to display the coloured vegetables. Slide onto a hot plate and serve at once.

raisin oatmeal muffins

Makes 24

125 g (4 oz) plain flour
3 teaspoons baking powder
¼ teaspoon salt
60 g (2 oz) butter
100 g (3½ oz) rolled oats
2 tablespoons caster sugar

125 g (4 oz) brown sugar, firmly packed
125 g (4 oz) raisins
250 ml (1 cup) milk
1 egg, beaten
½ teaspoon cinnamon

Preheat oven to 200°C (400°F). Sift flour, baking powder and salt together into a bowl, then rub in butter with your fingertips, until mixture resembles fine breadcrumbs. Add rolled oats, brown sugar, raisins, milk and egg, and mix well.

In a cup, combine sugar and cinnamon.

Pour mixture into deep, greased patty pans so that they are all three-quarters full, and sprinkle lightly with cinnamon sugar.

Bake in the oven for 18–20 minutes, or until a skewer inserted into the middle of the muffin comes out clean.

banana pancakes

Makes approx 8-10 small pancakes

1 cup (8 oz) plain (all-purpose) flour
2 teaspoons baking powder
2 tablespoons caster (superfine) sugar
1 egg, lightly beaten

1 ripe banana, small, mashed
30 g (1 oz) butter, melted
½ cup (4 fl oz)) milk
extra butter for frying

Place the flour, baking powder and sugar in a large bowl and stir to combine.

Combine the egg, banana, butter and milk together in another bowl.

Pour the wet ingredients into the dry and stir gently to combine.

Melt some butter in a frypan and spoon some pancake batter into the pan then tilt the pan so that the batter spreads out a little (make them as big or small as you like(. When the underside is lightly browned and there are bubbles forming on the top of the pancake, turn it over. Cook for a few more minutes until it is browned on the second side. You may need to adjust the temperature if it's browning too quickly or too slowly (the first pancake is normally a dud, so don't be disheartened).

Place the cooked pancake on a plate then repeat with the remaining batter. You'll need a little more butter in the pan before you make each pancake.

Allow the pancakes to cool.

rise and shine muesli muffins

Makes approx 24 mini muffins

1¼ cups (11 oz) self-raising (self-rising) flour	1 egg
¼ cup (2 oz) brown sugar, firmly packed	1 cup (8 fl oz) milk
⅓ cup (3 oz) muesli, plus extra for topping	60g (2 oz) butter, melted

Preheat oven to 180°C (350°F).

Grease a 24-hole mini muffin tray (or 12-hole regular muffin tray) or line with muffin papers.

In a large bowl combine the flour, sugar and muesli. In a medium-sized bowl combine the egg, milk and melted butter.

Pour the wet ingredients into the dry and mix gently until combined.

Spoon into the muffin holes, filling them to three- quarters full. Scatter a small amount of extra muesli over the top of each muffin. Bake in preheated oven for 10–12 minutes (or 20 minutes for regular muffin tray), until a skewer inserted in the middle comes out cleanly.

Mini muffins are often cooked in the middle but not brown on top. Place under a hot grill (broiler) for a minute or two until lightly browned (watch closely so they don't burn). Allow to cool.

You can easily substitute muesli with a mixture of rolled oats, coconut (desiccated or shredded) and dried fruit

toasted english muffins with bacon and cheese

4 bacon rashers, rind and most fat removed | 1 tablespoon tomato paste
2 English muffins | ½ cup cheddar, grated

Cut the bacon into bite-size pieces then cook in a frypan until slightly crispy. Drain on a plate covered with paper towelling. Split the muffins in half through the middle then toast both sides lightly under the grill (broiler) or in the toaster. Spread the cut side of each muffin with some tomato paste (don't use more than one tablespoon between the four muffin halves otherwise they will go soggy). Top with bacon pieces then scatter cheese over the top.

Place under the grill briefly to allow the cheese to melt.

Allow to cool.

These are a little like mini pizzas but with breakfast ingredients. They are quite simple- only four ingredients. Whip up some of these muffins and you'll have a few easy breakfasts up your sleeve.

homemade baked beans

Serves 3

olive oil	400 g (14 oz) tin Roma tomatoes, chopped
1 onion, finely chopped	1 tablespoon brown sugar
100 g (3½ oz) bacon, rind removed, finely diced	1 tablespoon Worcestershire sauce
400 g (14 oz) tin cannellini beans, drained and rinsed	1 teaspoon Dijon mustard

Heat some oil in a large saucepan over low-medium heat then add onion and bacon.

Cook for a few minutes or until the onion is translucent and bacon is a little bit crispy. Add remaining ingredients and stir to combine. Simmer uncovered over low heat for about 20-30 minutes, or until the beans are tender and the sauce is thick. Stir regularly so that it doesn't burn on the bottom.

Allow to cool.

vegetable fritters

1 carrot, peeled and grated
1 zucchini (courgette), grated
200 g (7 oz) sweet potato (kumara),peeled and grated
handful basil, chopped

⅓ cup cheddar or parmesan, finely grated
¼ cup (2 oz) plain (all purpose) flour
2 eggs, lightly beaten
olive oil

Combine all ingredients except eggs and oil in a large bowl. Add eggs and mix well to combine.

Heat some oil in a large frypan over medium heat. Place spoonfuls of mixture into the pan—cook three or four at a time. Use the back of the spoon to flatten the fritter mixture so that they're not too thick.

Cook for a few minutes on each side or until well browned. Remove the fritters to a cake rack to cool while you make the next batch. You'll need to add some more oil between batches. Allow to cool.

fruity bircher muesli

Serves 1

½–1 cup oats, soaked overnight if needed	2 tablespoons natural plain yoghurt
1 tablespoon organic currants	1 teaspoon honey
1 apple or firm pear	1 tablespoon mixed nuts and seeds
lemon or orange	pinch of cinnamon or fresh ginger powder

Soak the oats with the currants the night before or for an hour in a little water or fruit juice.

Combine grated apple or pear with a squeeze of lemon juice and one or two tablespoons of natural plain yoghurt.

Drizzle with honey and sprinkle with chopped nuts and cinnamon or ginger.

This recipe uses apple or pear, but you can use almost any other fruit. Add sliced or mashed banana, or a handful of fresh berries, or some chopped dried fruit such as apricots, dates, figs, pears, sultanas or raisins to change the flavour.

grilled banana on jam toast

Serves 4

4 slices rye or soy and linseed bread
4 teaspoons spreadable fruit
(no-cane-sugar-added spread)

2 large, ripe bananas
4 tablespoons no-fat/low-fat fruit yoghurt

Brown the toast on one side.
  Spoon the spread evenly over the non-browned side of the toast.
  Top with banana slices or mash the banana onto the spread side of each piece of bread.
  Grill the bananas until they are lightly browned.
  Serve topped with a tablespoon of your favourite no-fat or low-fat yoghurt

brunch

poached eggs with spinach and cheese

Serves 4

315 g (10 oz) packet frozen spinach	4 eggs
15 g (½ oz) butter	4 slices bread
salt and freshly ground black pepper, to taste	French mustard
pinch of ground nutmeg	1 tablespoon parmesan cheese, grated
1 tablespoon vinegar	

Cook spinach as directed. Drain between two plates, chop if necessary, return to saucepan and toss with butter, salt and pepper and nutmeg. Keep hot.

To poach eggs, heat about 5 cm (2 in) water in a frying pan until water is simmering.

Add vinegar; this helps eggs retain the desired shape. Break an egg into a saucer, swirl the pan water with a wooden spoon, and slide the egg very carefully into the centre of the 'swirl'.

Immediately lift the white over the yolk two or three times. Add the other eggs in the same manner. After 4 minutes, the white should appear just set. Remove eggs carefully with a drainer spoon, and transfer to a bowl of cold water, to release any vinegar and prevent further cooking.

Toast bread and spread lightly with French mustard. Arrange spinach on rounds of toast and make a slight cavity to hold poached egg. Drain egg and place in the centre, sprinkle with parmesan cheese and place under a hot grill until cheese has melted. Serve at once.

Note: Eggs for poaching should be very fresh.

wholemeal pancakes and cinnamon peaches

Makes 12 pancakes

2 cups (16 oz) wholemeal self-raising flour
2 cups skim milk
1 teaspoon canola oil
1 teaspoon vanilla essence
2 egg whites, beaten until stiff

410 g (14½ oz) can sliced peaches, in their own juice
1 teaspoon ground cinnamon
spray canola oil for cooking

Mix the flour with milk and oil in a suitable bowl. When combined fold in the egg whites and let sit for 5 minutes.

Heat the peaches in their juice with the cinnamon in the microwave until warm.

Spray a crepe or pancake pan with minimal oil and cook each pancake. Turn when the bubbles start to appear. Flip over and cook through.

Serve the pancakes with peaches and syrup over the top.

These are great served with flavoured non-fat yoghurt and straw¬berries too. The pancakes can be used for savoury meals too; try them for lunch topped with cold meats and salads; as they stay moist and carry flavour really well.

rolled oats, barley bran and stewed ginger apples

Serves 6

4 medium eating apples (Bonza, Fuji, Burnbrae, etc.)
1 x 4cm-long (1.5 in) piece root ginger
2 cups (16 oz) organic or original rolled oats
3 cups (24 fl oz) water

1 cup (8 fl oz) skim milk
2 tablespoons psyllium
4 tablespoons barley bran
4 tablespoons honey, preferably organic or yellow box

Cut the apples into quarters or eight wedges if larger and remove the core. Put into a saucepan and cover them with water. Slice the ginger finely and add to the apples. Cook at a simmer for 10 minutes. Remove from heat and cool in cooking juices.

Cook the oats with the water and milk. Simmer until tender for around 5 minutes.

Pour oats out into six individual serving bowls. Top with equal amounts of psyllium, bran, honey and stewed apple to serve.

You can add more milk if you want or even flavoured, non-fat yoghurt.

The apples keep for up to a week if you want to make more than this recipe. The ginger should be washed and scraped, not peeled.

cornbread, served with scrambled eggs and bacon

Makes 1 large loaf (approx 10-11 thick slices)

olive oil
5 large spring onions (scallions), finely chopped
1 cup plain (all-purpose) flour
100 g (3½ oz) polenta
2 teaspoons bicarbonate of soda (baking soda)
sea salt and pepper

handful parsley, chopped
2 eggs
¼ cup (60 ml) vegetable oil
½ cup (125 ml) sour cream
2 tablespoon (40 ml) milk
300 g (10 oz) tin of corn kernels, drained

Preheat oven to 180°C (350°F). Grease and line a 13 x 23 cm (5 x 9 in) loaf tin.

Heat some oil in a frypan and add spring onions. Cook over medium heat for a few minutes until soft. Set aside to cool. In a large bowl, combine the flour, polenta, bicarb soda, salt, pepper and parsley.

In a smaller bowl whisk together the eggs, oil, sour cream and milk then add corn and cooked spring onions. Stir to combine. Pour the wet ingredients over the dry ingredients and stir gently until well mixed.

Pour into prepared tin then bake in oven for 30-40 mins, or until a skewer inserted in the middle comes out cleanly. Leave in the tin for at least 10 minutes before turning out.

Toast the slices under a hot grill (broiler) (or grill carefully on the barbecue) then serve with your own version of scrambled eggs and bacon.

Here's something different to serve with eggs and bacon when you have guests for brunch. If you want an easy, casual meal you can cook scrambled eggs in a saucepan on the barbecue and grill the bacon and slices of cornbread next to the eggs. Cook the cornbread over a very low heat so they don't burn.

toasted nuts with strawberry puree and yoghurt

Serves 2

1 tablespoon almonds	1 punnet strawberries
1 tablespoon sunflower seeds	1 tablespoon honey
1 tablespoon sesame seeds	1 teaspoon cinnamon
1 tablespoon pepitas	1 cup goats milk yoghurt
1 tablespoon walnuts	

Preheat oven to 120°C (250°F). Place all the nuts on an oven tray and bake for 5-10 minutes or until slightly golden brown.

Place the strawberries, honey and cinnamon in a blender or food processor and blend until smooth.

To serve, divide the yoghurt between two serving bowls, pour the strawberry puree over the top then sprinkle with the nuts.

corn capsicum fritters with slow roast tomatoes

Makes 8-10 fritters

2 cobs of corn
olive oil
½ red capsicum (bell pepper), diced
1 cup (8 oz) plain (all-purpose) flour
1 teaspoon baking powder
pinch sea salt and black pepper
¼-½ teasp dried chilli flakes (optional)
2 eggs, lightly beaten
170 ml (6 fl oz) milk
small handful of fresh coriander (cilantro),
roughly chopped

SLOW ROAST TOMATOES
6 Roma tomatoes, cut in half length-wise
1 tablespoon olive oil
1 tablespoon Balsamic vinegar

With a sharp knife remove the kernels from the corn cobs. Heat some oil in a large frypan over medium heat and cook the corn kernels and capsicum for a few minutes until they are tender and some of the corn is lightly browned. Allow to cool.

In a large bowl combine the flour, baking powder, salt, pepper and chilli flakes (if using).

In another bowl, combine the eggs, milk, coriander, corn and capsicum. Pour the wet ingredients over the dry ingredients and mix gently until well combined.

Heat some oil in a large frypan over medium heat and add a spoonful of the batter for each fritter, spreading the batter out a little with the back of a spoon. When the underside is cooked turn them over and cook the second side. You should be able to cook a few at a time if you make them about 8-10 cm (3-4 in) in diameter. As they are done remove them to a plate or cake rack and allow to cool. Repeat with remaining batter.

SLOW ROAST TOMATOES

Preheat oven to 180°C (350°F). Line a baking tray with baking paper. Place tomatoes on the tray then brush the cut side with the combined oil and vinegar. Bake in oven for 15 mins then drop the temperature to 150°C (300°F) and continue cooking for another 60-70 mins. Allow to cool.

Serve by making a sandwich from two fritters with some tomatoes and a few rocket (arugula) leaves.

banana bread with oat and almond topping

Makes 1 large loaf (about 10–11 thick slices)

125 g (4½ oz) butter, softened
120 g (4 oz) caster (superfine) sugar
2 eggs
3 large, ripe bananas, mashed
250 g (9 oz) plain (all-purpose) flour
2 teaspoons baking powder
½ teaspoon cinnamon
¼ cup sultanas (or chopped raisins)

TOPPING
2 tablespoons rolled oats
2 tablespoons flaked or slivered almonds

Preheat oven to 180°C (350°F). Grease and line a 13 x 23 cm (5 x 9 in) loaf tin.

Cream butter and sugar until light and fluffy, then add eggs one at a time, beating well after each addition.

Add mashed banana and stir until thoroughly combined.

Sift flour, baking powder and cinnamon together then add to the banana mixture. Stir gently to combine, then add sultanas (raisins) and stir them in too.

Pour into prepared tin, smooth the top with a spatula then scatter the oats and almonds over the top, pressing them in lightly so they'll stick.

Bake in oven for 50-60 mins, or until a skewer inserted in the middle comes out cleanly.

Serve with butter. You can serve as is or toast lightly under the grill (broiler). If grilling, watch carefully as the topping may burn so you may need to drape some foil over the topping.

cinnamon waffles with caramelised apples and maple syrup

Serves 4

200 g (6½ oz) plain (all-purpose) flour
1 teaspoon baking powder
2 teaspoons cinnamon
80 g (3 oz) caster (superfine) sugar
1 cup (8 fl oz) milk
2 eggs
90 g (3 oz) butter, melted and cooled slightly
4 green apples, peeled and sliced thickly
30 g (1 oz) butter
2 tablespoons sugar (or more if apples are sour)

TO SERVE
maple syrup
mascarpone (optional)

Preheat waffle iron according to the manufacturer's instructions. Sift the flour, baking powder and cinnamon into a large bowl then add sugar. Stir to combine. In a smaller bowl whisk together the milk, eggs and melted butter.

Pour the wet ingredients over the dry ingredients and stir gently until combined.

Spoon some batter into the waffle iron and spread it with the back of the spoon to within 2cm (1 in) of the edge.

Cook the waffle according to the manufacturer's instructions. Once cooked, remove the waffle and allow to cool on a cake rack. Repeat with remaining batter.

CARAMELISED APPLES

Melt butter in a large frypan over low-medium heat then add apples. Cook for 10 minutes, add sugar, then cook for another 5-10 minutes. You want them to be soft but not mushy. Allow to cool.

Place a waffle on each plate, top with a dollop of mascarpone and apples, then drizzle maple syrup.

scrambled eggs and smoked salmon and baby spinach

Serves 2

4 eggs	2 large bunches of baby spinach leaves or small
½ cup (4 fl oz) milk and ¼ cup (2 fl oz) of	English spinach leaves, cut in half
thickened cream	2 slices smoked salmon, cut into thin strips
(can use light or skim)	juice of half a lemon
olive oil	cracked black pepper

Beat the eggs with the milk and the cream in a bowl. Heat the olive oil in a heavy pan and turn it to a low heat. Pour in the egg mixture. Immediately sprinkle the spinach leaves into the pan. Stir slowly until the eggs begin to thicken. Add the smoked salmon evenly over the pan. When thick, serve with a sprinkle of lemon juice and plenty of cracked pepper.

scrambled tofu

Serves 2

¼ red onion
¼ cup (2 oz) mushrooms
¼ cup (2 oz) cherry tomato, chopped in halves
1 cup (8 oz)organic hard tofu, crumbled

1 garlic clove, crushed
small handful of basil or flat leaf parsley
½ teaspoon fresh chilli

Sauté the Spanish onion, garlic, mushrooms and tomatoes in a frying pan for about 5 minutes.

Add the tofu, chilli and basil into saucepan with the onion mixture and cook until heated through for approximately 7 minutes.

Serve with a drizzle of extra virgin olive oil and season.

raw berry porridge

Serves 1

1 cup (8 fl oz) milk	1 cup (8 oz) berries
1 cup (8 oz) rolled oats	½ banana
1 tablespoon psyllium husks	1 scoop whey protein powder (optional)

Place all the ingredients into a food processor and blend until smooth. Serve in either a bowl or glass.

hard boiled egg with sea salt and chilli mix

1-2 hard boiled eggs	1 teaspoon chilli powder
1 teaspoon sea salt	

Place the salt and chilli in a small bowl and mix together. Chop the hard boiled eggs in half and then dip the flat side into the chilli mix.

Serve salt side up on a plate.

toad in the hole

Serves 4-6

8 thick pork or beef sausages
1 tablespoon butter
1 quantity Yorkshire Pudding batter

YORKSHIRE PUDDING BATTER
250 g (8 oz) plain flour
pinch of salt
1 egg
315 ml (11 oz) milk

FOR THE PUDDING:
Preheat oven to 250°C (485°F). Sift flour and salt together into a bowl. Make a well in the centre and drop egg in. Add half the milk, a little at a time, and gradually stir in the flour from the sides of the bowl, using a wooden spoon. Mix until smooth, then beat batter with the back of the spoon for 5-10 minutes.

When thoroughly beaten, air bubbles appear on the surface. Cover batter and allow to stand for 30 minutes.

Preheat oven to 220°C (420°F). Place oven shelf just above centre. Place sausages in a baking dish with butter.

Heat in the oven until fat is very hot.

Pour in Yorkshire Pudding batter quickly and bake for 20-35 minutes, or until batter is well risen, crisp and browned.

Serve with seasonal vegetables.

crêpes

Serves 4-6

125 g (4 oz) self-raising flour
pinch of salt
½ teaspoon bicarbonate of soda
1 cup (8 fl oz) milk

3 tablespoons caster sugar
1 egg
butter, for cooking

Place flour, salt, bicarbonate of soda, milk, sugar and egg in a jug and beat together until there are no lumps.

Heat a frying pan on low, and add enough butter to cover the bottom liberally. As the pan heats, tilt it to allow butter to run all over the surface. Drain off extra butter, leaving just a film in the pan.

Off the heat, pour in enough batter to run all over pan bottom—about 1 tablespoon for a pan 15 cm (6 in) across.

Replace pan over heat and cook until the upper surface of the crepe appears bubbly. Run a small spatula around the edge to loosen the crêpe, then slide the knife under and turn or toss crepe over.

The side cooked first is served as the outer side.

Turn finished crêpes on to a wire rack and cover with a clean tea towel. Stack slightly overlapping and wrap to keep warm.

Serve with jam and freshly whipped cream or lemon juice and sugar.

sandwiches and wraps

blt

Serves 4

1 tablespoon olive oil
8 rashers bacon, rind removed
8 slices wholemeal bread, buttered
3 tablespoons mayonnaise

4 small tomatoes, sliced
4 iceberg lettuce leaves
freshly ground black pepper, to taste

Place oil in a frying pan and cook bacon until crisp.

Spread four slices of the bread or toast with mayonnaise. Top each slice with a lettuce leaf, tomato slices and two rashers of bacon. Add pepper, close with remaining slices of bread and serve.

chicken salad sandwich

Serves 2

4 slices mixed grain bread
1 tablespoon margarine
2 tablespoons mayonnaise
80 g (3 oz) lean chicken breast,
cooked and shredded

1 small tomato, sliced
1 small cucumber, sliced
½ cup bean sprouts
2 iceberg lettuce leaves

Lightly spread two slices of bread with margarine and mayonnaise. Top each slice with chicken, tomato, cucumber, bean sprouts and a lettuce leaf and close with remaining bread.

cottage cheese
and salmon sandwich

Serves 2

½ cup (4 oz) cottage cheese | 4 slices mixed grain bread
180 g (6 oz) can salmon in brine, drained | 1 tablespoon margarine

In a small bowl, gently combine cottage cheese and salmon. Lightly spread two slices of bread with margarine, pile on cottage cheese and salmon and close with remaining bread.

greek salad wrap

Serves 4

4 large pieces pitta bread | 2 medium tomatoes, seeded and finely chopped
250 g (8 oz) tub tzatziki | 50 g (2 oz) black olives, seeded and sliced
1 Lebanese cucumber, seeded and finely chopped | ½ small red (Spanish) onion, sliced
100 g (3 oz) fetta cheese, crumbled | 1 tablespoon fresh mint leaves, roughly chopped

Spread one side of pitta bread with tzatziki, top with remaining ingredients and roll up.

grilled ham, cheese and tomato sandwich

Serves 4

8 slices wholegrain bread	8 thin slices ham
3 tablespoons margarine	4 thin slices cheddar cheese
2 small tomatoes, sliced	salt and freshly ground black pepper, to taste

Spread a little margarine over slices of bread. Top four bread slices with tomato, two slices of ham and one slice of cheese. Season with salt and pepper. Top with remaining bread slices and place in a sandwich grill for about three minutes or until golden brown. Cut in half and serve.

roast beef sandwich

Serves 4

8 slices rye bread	2 small tomatoes, sliced
3 tablespoons margarine	½ red onion, sliced
2 teaspoons horseradish	4 iceberg lettuce leaves
4 slices roast beef	freshly ground black pepper, to taste
4 slices Swiss cheese	

Spread margarine, then horseradish on four bread slices. Top each with slice of roast beef, slice of Swiss cheese, tomato, onion and a lettuce leaf. Cover with remaining slices of bread and serve.

veggie wrap

Serves 4

125 g (4 oz) cream cheese	2 carrots, peeled and grated
4 flour tortillas	4 large white mushrooms, sliced
1 cucumber, peeled and thinly sliced	1 clove garlic, chopped
2 small tomatoes, thinly sliced	

Thinly spread one tablespoon cream cheese on each tortilla. Place some cucumber, tomato, carrot and mushroom evenly across centre of tortilla. Roll up tortilla, trapping ingredients tightly inside to form a tight tube. Slice each tube into 2.5 cm (1 in) sections to serve.

roast vegetable focaccia

Serves 4

1 eggplant (aubergine), sliced into strips
2 red capsicums (bell peppers), halved
2 tablespoons olive oil
2 large white mushrooms, sliced

3 cloves garlic, crushed
4 tablespoons mayonnaise
1 long loaf focaccia

Place eggplant and capsicum skin side up under a preheated grill and cook for 10 minutes or until flesh is soft and skins are blackened. Peel away blackened skin and roughly chop flesh.

Heat one tablespoon of the olive oil and sauté mushrooms until tender.

Stir crushed garlic into mayonnaise.

Slice focaccia in half lengthwise. Spread mayonnaise mixture on one or both halves.

Arrange eggplant, capsicum and mushrooms on one focaccia half, place other half on top. Cut loaf into four equal portions. To toast and flatten sandwich, place in a sandwich grill until golden, and serve.

toasted mexican rollups with spiked sour cream

Serves 3

2 pieces tortillas bread	SPIKED SOUR CREAM
¼ cup refried beans or mashed chilli beans	2 tablespoons light sour cream
1 cup tasty cheese, grated	½ teaspoon chilli powder
1 avocado, peeled and de-stoned	1 teaspoon lime or lemon juice
1 cup tomato salsa	
olive oil	

Preheat oven to 190°C (375°F).

Lay naan bread on a board and spread with refried or mashed chilli beans to within 1 cm (½ in) of the edge.

Sprinkle over cheese.

Mash avocado flesh with tomato salsa. Spread over cheese. Roll up bread and brush with olive oil.

Bake rolls in the oven for 10 minutes or until crisp and golden. Cut one-third of the roll on the diagonal and spoon over spiked sour cream.

To make spiked sour cream, mix all ingredients in a bowl until well combined.

tuna and mayonnaise wrap

Serves 4

1 stick celery, finely chopped
425 g (14 oz) can tuna in brine,
drained and flaked
¼ cup (2 oz) mayonnaise

⅓ cup fresh coriander (cilantro) leaves, chopped
1 tablespoon lemon juice
4 pieces lavash bread
1 small cos lettuce, torn

Combine celery, tuna, mayonnaise, coriander and lemon juice in a medium bowl. Top bread with lettuce, then with tuna mixture. Roll up from the short side and serve.

turkey salad sandwich

Serves 2

4 slices multigrain bread
1 tablespoon margarine
90 g (3 oz) lean turkey breast

150 g (6 oz) mixed salad leaves
(cos/Romaine lettuce, rocket, iceberg lettuce)
salt and freshly ground black pepper, to taste

Lightly spread two slices of bread with margarine. Top bread with turkey, salad leaves, salt and pepper and cover with remaining slices of bread.

barbecued chicken wraps

Serves 4

¼ cup (2 oz) low-fat natural yoghurt
1 teaspoon lemon juice
2 teaspoons Dijon mustard
4 pieces lavash bread
4 cups cos (Romaine) lettuce leaves, shredded

1 red capsicum (bell pepper), sliced thinly
12 green beans, blanched and chopped diagonally
½ red onion, sliced
400 g (13 oz) barbecued chicken breast or thigh, cut into bite-sized pieces

Combine yoghurt, lemon juice and mustard and spread over one side of the lavash bread. Lay salad ingredients along a short side and place chicken on top. Roll up, wrap in a serviette and eat immediately.

soups and light meals

calamari rings in tempura batter

Serves 6

750 g (1½ lb) squid tubes (squid hoods)
olive oil, for deep frying

BATTER
60 g (2 oz) plain (all-purpose) flour
60 g (2 oz) cornflour (cornstarch)
1 teaspoon baking powder (see glossary)
pinch of salt
pinch of freshly ground black pepper
1 cup (8 fl oz) cold water

Cut squid tubes into 5 mm (¼ in) rings. Place rings on absorbent paper and dry well.

Sift plain flour, cornflour and baking powder into a bowl. Add salt and pepper. Gradually add water and beat lightly — it doesn't matter if the mixture remains slightly lumpy.

Heat oil to smoking point (it may spit and splatter, so be careful). Dip squid rings into batter, allow to drain slightly, and place in oil. Cook until lightly golden (three minutes maximum). Drain well and serve hot with tartare sauce or seafood sauce.

chicken and mushroom vol-au-vents

Serves 2

2 chicken stock cubes	500 g (1 lb) chicken breast fillets,
60 g (2 oz) sour cream	cooked and chopped
30 g (1 oz) butter	1 x 190 g (6 oz) can champignons,
2 tablespoons plain (all-purpose) flour	drained (see glossary)
1¼ cups (10 fl oz) milk	salt and black pepper, to taste
	4 individual ready-baked vol-au-vent cases

Preheat oven to 180°C (350°F).

In a bowl, crumble chicken stock cubes and mix with sour cream.

In a saucepan, melt butter and stir in flour until smooth. Cook for about two minutes. Add milk and stir continuously, bringing to the boil. Add sour cream mixture, chopped chicken and champignons. Season with salt and pepper and cook until mixture is heated through and sour cream has melted into a sauce.

Fill vol-au-vent cases with mixture and place on a baking tray. Bake in the oven for 15–20 minutes. Serve piping hot with a green salad.

chicken noodle soup

Serves 4-6

3⅔ cups (28 fl oz) chicken stock
1 bay leaf (see glossary)
1 onion, halved

250 g (8 oz) skinless chicken breast, whole
60 g (2 oz) vermicelli, broken into smaller pieces
salt and freshly ground black pepper, to taste
1 tablespoon fresh parsley, chopped, to garnish

Place chicken stock, bay leaf, onion and chicken breast into a large saucepan over a high heat. Heat to boiling, stirring once or twice. Reduce heat to a simmer and cook for 10 minutes or until chicken is tender and cooked through.

Lift chicken out of the saucepan with a draining spoon and cut into very small pieces. Remove onion and bay leaf and discard. Strain stock and return to cleaned saucepan. Bring stock back to the boil, add vermicelli and cook for seven minutes or until al dente. Return chopped chicken to saucepan, season with salt and pepper, then heat through.

Ladle into warm soup bowls and sprinkle with chopped parsley to serve.

garlic prawns

Serves 12 as an appetiser, 8 as an entrée

½ cup (4 fl oz) olive oil
4 large cloves garlic, peeled
1 tablespoon parsley, chopped

½ teaspoon salt
1 kg (2 lb) small green prawns (shrimps),
peeled and deveined

In a bowl, combine oil, garlic, parsley and salt. Add prawns, cover and let stand for two hours in the refrigerator.

Preheat oven to 250°C (485°F). Place prawns and marinade in an ovenproof casserole dish and cook for 10 minutes, or until prawns turn pink. Remove garlic cloves.

Serve as an appetiser on cocktail sticks, or as an entrée in small ramekins.

chicken satay sticks

Serves 2

few drops soy sauce
few drops Tabasco sauce
1 teaspoon white vinegar
1 teaspoon oil
1 teaspoon brown sugar

1 clove garlic
185 g (6 oz) chicken breast,
cut into 1 cm (½ in) cubes
bamboo skewers, soaked in water

In a bowl, combine soy sauce, Tabasco sauce, white vinegar, oil, brown sugar and garlic. Put chicken cubes into bowl, cover and marinate for at least two hours in the refrigerator.

Put chicken cubes on skewers and cook very quickly under a hot grill. Serve on the skewers accompanied by a bed of rice.

guacamole

Serves 8

2 tablespoons lemon juice
2–3 tablespoons olive oil
½ clove garlic, peeled and crushed
salt, to taste
½ teaspoon Tabasco sauce

1 large avocado, diced
2 heaped tablespoons sour cream
1 small onion, finely chopped
1 tomato, diced

Place all ingredients except onion and tomato in a bowl and beat together with a fork until a smooth consistency is reached. Add tomato and onion and mix through. Serve with corn chips.

crab bisque

Serves 6

250 g (8 oz) fresh or canned crabmeat
60 g (2 oz) butter
4 tablespoons plain (all-purpose) flour
1.25 L (40 fl oz) milk, scalded (see glossary)
pinch of freshly grated nutmeg

salt and freshly ground black pepper, to taste
4 tablespoons dry sherry
1 tablespoon whipped cream, to garnish
1 teaspoon paprika, to garnish

Flake crabmeat and pass it through a food processor or blender.

Make a roux by melting butter in a saucepan and blending in flour until smooth. Cook for about three minutes. Add milk and stir sauce continuously, until thick and smooth. Add nutmeg and season with salt and pepper. Cook gently for 12-15 minutes. Add prepared crabmeat and continue cooking for a further five minutes. Just before serving, stir in sherry. Serve hot or cold, top with whipped cream and paprika.

cream of mushroom soup

Serves 4

250 g (8 oz) mushrooms
125 g (4 oz) butter
½ teaspoon salt
freshly ground black pepper, to taste

3 cloves garlic, finely chopped
1.25 L (40 fl oz) chicken stock
½ cup (4 fl oz) fresh cream,
at room temperature

Before cooking mushrooms, select some of the smallest ones and take a slice from the centre of each so that you have the outline of the mushroom. Put aside.

Wash mushrooms (do not peel them), remove stalks and chop coarsely. In a frying pan, heat butter to sizzling, then fry mushrooms with salt and a good grind of fresh pepper. Cool, then purée in a blender or food processor with garlic and 250 ml (8½ fl oz) of the stock.

Pour remaining stock into a large saucepan. Add mushroom purée and heat to simmering point. Stir in cream. Add reserved mushroom slices and simmer soup for five minutes. Serve hot with crusty bread.

sweet corn and ham flan

Serves 6

1 x 375 g (12 oz) packet short-crust pastry
egg white

FILLING
30 g (1 oz) butter
2 tablespoons onion, chopped
1 x 270 g (9 oz) can whole-kernel
sweet corn, drained
1 tablespoon fresh parsley, chopped
3 eggs
1 teaspoon salt
pinch of freshly ground black pepper
1 cup (8 fl oz) fresh cream
60 g (2 oz) ham, thinly sliced
90 g (3 oz) tasty cheese, thinly sliced

Preheat oven to 180°C (350°F). Roll out pastry on a lightly floured board and line a 20 cm (8 in) flan tin. Brush the pastry with a little egg white.

To make the filling, melt butter in a small saucepan and cook onion on a moderate heat, without browning, for two minutes. In a bowl, mix onion with sweet corn and parsley and spread over pastry. In a separate bowl, beat eggs lightly with salt and pepper. In another saucepan, heat cream until lukewarm, then add it to eggs, combine, and pour over sweet corn. Top with slices of ham and cheese.

Bake for 30–35 minutes, or until pastry is golden brown and the filling is set in the centre.

creamy chicken and vegetable soup

Serves 4-6

1 x 1.5 kg (3 lb) cooked roast chicken carcass	salt and freshly ground black pepper, to taste
3⅔ cups (28 fl oz) water	4 tablespoons fresh cream
1 bay leaf	2 tablespoons plain (all-purpose) flour
1 chicken stock cube	125 g (4 oz) mixed vegetables (potatoes, carrot, celery and parsnip), cooked and chopped

Break chicken carcass into pieces and place in a large saucepan. Cover with water, add bay leaf, stock cube and salt and pepper. Bring to the boil over a high heat, then turn heat down to a simmer. Add cream and flour, stir through, cover with a lid and cook for one hour.

Discard chicken carcass and bay leaf. Drain contents of saucepan through a colander into a large bowl, then return liquid to the saucepan. Add cooked vegetables to the liquid. Cook gently for five minutes and serve.

hamburgers

Serves 6

1 small onion, grated
500 g (1 lb) minced (ground) beef
3 tablespoons plain (all-purpose) flour
¼ cup (2 fl oz) milk

125 g (4 oz) plain (all-purpose) flour
¼ cup (2 fl oz) olive oil
6 hamburger buns
tasty chesse, sliced
tomatoes, sliced
beetroot (beets), sliced
lettuce, shredded
pickles, sliced

Mix onion and meat thoroughly in a bowl using a wooden spoon. Add three tablespoons of flour and mix in thoroughly. Pour milk over meat mixture and stir in well.

Place extra flour in a small bowl. Divide meat mixture into six balls and roll each one in flour until well coated. Lift it out onto a plate and flatten it slightly. Continue until all the meat is used.

Pour oil into a frying pan and place over a medium heat. When the oil starts to bubble, gently place hamburger patties in the pan. Cook until the bottoms of the hamburgers are brown, then flip them over and cook until they are brown on the other side. Drain patties on absorbent paper. (They can also be grilled or barbecued.)

Place patties on hamburger buns and add tomato sauce, sliced tasty cheese, sliced tomatoes, sliced beetroot (beets), sliced pickles, cooked sliced onion and shredded lettuce.

lamb kebabs

Serves 6

1 x 2 kg (4 lb) lamb shoulder, boned	6 bamboo skewers,
500 g (1 lb) small onions	(soak in water for 10 minutes before using)
1 green capsicum (bell pepper),	6 small tomatoes
pith and seeds removed	bay leaves (optional)
2 rashers bacon, rind removed	salt and freshly ground black pepper, to taste
6-12 button mushrooms	olive oil or melted butter

Cut lamb into 2.5 cm (1 in) cubes. Peel onions and blanch in boiling water, then drain. Cut capsicum and bacon into 2.5 cm (1 in) pieces.

Thread lamb onto skewers alternately with onion, mushrooms, capsicum, bacon and tomatoes. Small bay leaves can be added if used. Season with salt and pepper and brush with oil. Grill gently, turning and brushing again with oil if necessary, for 20-25 minutes, or until meat is cooked.

Serve on a bed of steamed rice.

leek, potato and bacon soup

Serves 4-6

2.5 kg (5 lb) potatoes, peeled and cut into chunks
2 leeks, sliced into 2.5 cm (1 in) rings
500 g (1 lb) bacon, chopped
salt and freshly ground black pepper, to taste

300 g (10 oz) sour cream
¼ bunch shallots (green onions), chopped
½ bunch coriander (cilantro), chopped

Place potatoes in a large saucepan with enough cold water to cover. Bring water to the boil and cook potatoes for about 10 minutes or until soft. Drain, leaving a little water. Mash potatoes with the water (adding more if necessary). The mixture should have the consistency of thick soup. Add leek and bacon to the mashed potatoes and simmer until leek is soft and bacon is cooked. Season with salt and pepper.

In a bowl, mix sour cream and shallots and gently stir mixture into the soup. Reheat gently, not allowing the mixture to boil again (the sour cream will curdle if it boils). Serve hot, garnished with coriander.

*Variations: Add your favourite crunchy vegetable a few minutes before serving,
or crisp-fry the bacon and add it just before serving.*

mussels with garlic

Serves 4

1 large onion, finely chopped
2 cloves garlic, crushed
1 tablespoon fresh parsley, chopped, plus extra to garnish

2¼ cups (10 fl oz) white wine
salt and freshly ground black pepper, to taste
2 kg (4 lb) mussels in their shells, washed and debearded

Put onion, garlic, parsley, wine, salt and pepper in a large pot, bring to the boil, then simmer for five minutes. Add mussels, cover pot, and steam mussels, shaking the pan from time to time, for five minutes or until mussels have opened. Remove mussels from the pot, discarding any shells that have not opened.

Turn heat to high and reduce sauce.

Arrange mussels on a platter, spoon over sauce and garnish with extra parsley.

pumpkin soup

Serves 8

60 g (2 oz) butter
1 onion, finely chopped
2½ cups (1 pint) chicken stock
500 g (1 lb) pumpkin, peeled, seeded and cut into 5 cm (2 in) chunks

2½ cups (1 pint) hot milk
pinch of ground allspice (see glossary)
salt and freshly ground black pepper, to taste
125 ml (4 fl oz) thickened cream
finely chopped parsley, to garnish

Melt butter in a large saucepan and gently fry onion for five minutes, or until soft. Add chicken stock and bring to the boil. Add pumpkin and simmer until tender, about 30 minutes. Cool. Purée pumpkin in a food processor or blender. Return soup to pan, add hot milk, allspice, salt and pepper, and heat gently. Add thickened cream just before serving.

Serve in a tureen, lightly sprinkled with parsley.

salmon quiche

Serves 6

PASTRY	FILLING
60 g (2 oz) plain (all-purpose) flour, sifted	4 rashers bacon, rind removed and diced
60 g (2 oz) wholemeal flour	1 x 210 g (7 oz) can salmon in brine
½ teaspoon salt	3 eggs
90 g (3 oz) butter	1½ cups (12 fl oz) fresh cream
1 egg yolk	1 tablespoon parsley, chopped
1 tablespoon lemon juice	1 tablespoon Parmesan cheese, grated
	½ teaspoon paprika
	1 teaspoon salt
	freshly ground black pepper, to taste

Preheat oven to 200°C (400°F).

To make the pastry, mix flours and salt together in a bowl. Rub in butter with your fingertips, until mixture resembles fine breadcrumbs. Add egg yolk and lemon juice and mix to form a firm dough (if mixture appears too dry, add a tablespoon of water). Press the pastry into a greased 25 cm (10 in) flan tin.

To make the filling, gently fry bacon in a small frying pan. Drain on absorbent paper. Drain and flake salmon, reserving liquid. Arrange salmon on the base of the pastry, then sprinkle bacon on top.

In a bowl, beat together reserved salmon liquid, eggs, cream, parsley, cheese, paprika, salt and pepper. Pour mixture gently, over the back of a spoon, into the flan tin to cover salmon and bacon.

Bake for 10 minutes, then reduce heat to 165°C (325°F) and cook for a further 30–35 minutes, or until the filling is set.

savoury crêpes

Makes 12-16 small crêpes

250 g (8 oz) plain (all-purpose) flour	1 tablespoon oil
pinch of salt	1 cup (8 fl oz) milk
1 egg	¼ cup (2 fl oz) water
1 extra egg yolk	butter or oil, for cooking

Sift flour and salt into a bowl. Make a well in the centre and drop in the whole egg, extra egg yolk and oil. Using a wooden spoon, stir from the centre to blend egg and oil with flour. As the mixture thickens, add milk, a little at a time, stirring from the centre, and making bigger circular movements as more flour is incorporated. When all the flour is blended, beat well and add any remaining milk and the water. The resulting batter should be the consistency of thin cream. Strain, then cover and allow to stand for at least 30 minutes, to enable the starch cells in the flour to swell and soften. Stir thoroughly before using.

Heat crêpe pan a little, then add enough butter or oil to cover the bottom liberally. As the pan heats, tilt to allow butter or oil to run all over the surface. Drain off extra butter or oil, leaving just a film in the pan. Take the pan off the heat and pour in just enough batter to run all over the bottom of the pan – about 1 tablespoon for a 14-15 cm (5½-6 in) pan. Replace the pan on the heat and cook until upper surface of crêpe begins to bubble. Run a small spatula around to loosen edges, slide spatula under and turn crêpe over. The side cooked first is served as the outer side. Turn finished crêpe (the second side should take no more than two minutes to cook) onto a wire rack covered with a clean tea towel. Stack crêpes so that they overlap slightly, and wrap the tea towel around them to keep them warm.

Serve with barbecued chicken pieces and melted cheese or smoked salmon and melted cheese.

satay chicken triangles

Makes 30 triangles

3 small chicken breast fillets, finely diced
20 sheets filo pastry
butter, melted

MARINADE
¼ cup (2 fl oz) oil
2 tablespoons white wine vinegar
1 tablespoon teriyaki sauce
2 teaspoons sesame oil

PEANUT SAUCE
1 tablespoon tomato ketchup
2 teaspoons chilli sauce
125 g (4 oz) smooth peanut butter
⅓ cup (2¾ fl oz) chicken stock
2 teaspoons lemon juice

To make marinade, combine all marinade ingredients in a bowl. Add chicken and marinate for about four hours in the refrigerator.

Preheat oven to 220°C (420°F). Heat an electric frypan or wok, add chicken and half the marinade and stir-fry the chicken for 10 minutes or until golden.

Brush one sheet of filo pastry with melted butter and top with a second sheet of pastry. Cut pastry lengthwise into three strips. Spoon a portion of the filling into the corner of one end of a pastry strip. Fold pastry diagonally over filling, from one corner to the opposite side, to form a triangle. Continue to fold pastry, making a triangle every time, until whole strip is used. Brush triangle with butter on both sides and put on a baking tray. Repeat until all filling and all pastry sheets are used. Bake triangles in the oven for 15 minutes, or until pastry is golden brown and flaking.

In a saucepan, combine the ingredients for the peanut sauce and cook for two minutes. Allow to cool slightly before serving.

Serve with the peanut sauce for dipping.

paella

Serves 6

3 cups (1½ lb) long grain rice, cover with water
2 teaspoons veggie stock powder
2 teaspoons dried arame seaweed
pinch saffron or 1 teaspoon turmeric
sea salt and pepper, to taste
1 tablespoon olive oil
1 large brown onion, finely sliced
2 cloves garlic, crushed

1 green capsicum (bell pepper), chopped
2 carrots, diced
300 g packet vegan smoked sausage, diced
1 cup vegan fish pieces (available from Asian supermarkets)
2 zucchinis (courgettes), diced
1 cup peas
4 tomatoes, diced

Cover rice with water and bring to the boil. Add stock powder, seaweed, spice and seasoning and cook until the rice is cooked and water is absorbed.

Heat oil and add onion, garlic and capsicum for 5 minutes until soft. Add carrot and cook for a further 5 minutes.

Stir in remaining ingredients and cook for

15 minutes or until the vegetables are tender. Fold the rice through the vegetables and serve in a large bowl.

Paella, considered Spain's national dish, is made from rice and a variety of ingredients, usually seafood. This paella has been adapted for vegans.

salsa verde (green sauce)

1 bunch parsley	1 bunch basil
1 tablespoon capers	3 garlic cloves
¼ cup (2 fl oz)olive oil	1 teaspoon salt
1 bunch mint	1 bunch coriander
1 can anchovy fillets	1 tablespoon mustard
½ cup (4 fl oz) white wine vinegar	2 teaspoons peppercorns

Place all the ingredients into a food processor or blender and mix until combined.

This was originally a sauce for pork chops, but goes with any grills and roast meats.
It can also be used as a pesto, or mixed with mayonnaise to go with cold chicken and seafood.

cauliflower soup

1 cauliflower, broken up	1 carrot, chopped
1 large potato, peeled and cut into small pieces	1 container Sour Cream
chicken stock	salt and pepper to taste
1 large onion, chopped	

Boil the cauliflower and potato until soft in chicken stock, then mash.

Add the onion and carrot and simmer for 5–10 minutes, depending on the consistency you desire. Add the sour cream to the soup before serving.

You can easily vary this by adding 4 or more carrots to make it a predominantly carrot soup, add boiled chicken thighs, sprinkle finely-chopped eschalots or parsley on top when serving or serve with croutons.

smoked chicken and pea soup

1 smoked chicken
1 packet of split peas
1 packet of soup vegetables (parsnip, carrot,
onion, celery, swede, potato)

handful of coriander
salt and pepper to taste

Soak the split peas for 1 hour.

Boil the chicken, cool then de-bone and cut into small pieces that would be manageable with a spoon.

Boil the split peas until they begin to break, then add the diced soup vegetables. Once the split peas are fully broken, add the chicken and the chopped coriander.

Serve with coarse bread.

You can easily vary this by adding more of the vegetables such as mushroom, adding cream of sour cream, using fresh chicken thighs (trimmed of fat) instead of the smoked chicken.

vegetarian nachos

Serves 4 as entrée

200 g (6½ oz) packet of corn chips
425 g (15 oz) can mixed beans, drained
1 cup (8 fl oz) nachos sauce or home made salsa
2 cups grated cheddar cheese
½ cup (4 fl oz) light sour cream

2 tomatoes, chopped
1 small onion, finely chopped
1 avocado, peeled
juice of 1 lemon

Preheat oven to 180°C (350°F). Arrange the corn chips on either 1 large, or 4 individual heat resistant plates. Mix together the beans, sauce and cheese in a bowl. Pour the mixture over the middle of the corn chips.

Bake in oven for 10–15 minutes until cheese has melted and chips are golden. Mash together the avocado and the lemon juice.

Take out of the oven and drizzle with the sour cream. Top with the tomatoes and the onion and finally the avocado mixture.

Serve immediately.

bruscetta

Serves 4

8 roma tomatoes, finely chopped	4 slices of crusty bread, preferably Italian style
4 cloves fresh garlic, crushed	pinch salt and pepper to taste
olive oil	Parmesan cheese, finely grated

Mix the garlic into the chopped tomatoes in a bowl. Slice the bread and toast it on one side only. Brush the untoasted side with the olive oil and layer with tomatoes. Sprinkle with parmesan cheese and serve.

chicken, celery, apple and walnut with lime mayonnaise

Serves 4

2 cups (1 lb) skinless white chicken meat, diced	1 tablespoon chives, chopped
2 cups (1 lb) celery, diced	½ cup (4 fl oz) low-fat mayonnaise
1 cup (8 oz) apple, diced	½ cup (4 fl oz) lime juice
½ (4 oz) cup walnuts, roughly broken	ground white pepper to taste

Mix the chicken, celery, apple, walnuts and chives. Stir the mayo, lime and pepper together and pour over the chicken mix. Tumble well and serve immediately over shredded lettuce or mixed leaves.

bean, corn and spinach quesadillas

Serves 4

3 cups (1½ lb) well-packed baby spinach leaves
olive oil
1 onion, chopped
1 clove garlic, crushed
1 cup (8 oz) corn kernels, fresh or frozen
3 tablespoons tomato paste
2 tablespoons water
¼ teasp dried chilli flakes
8 large flour tortillas (20cm/8 in diameter)
400g (14 oz) tin refried beans
(you only need about half of the tin)
approx 1 cup (8 oz) grated cheddar cheese

TO SERVE
Tomato Salsa: diced, fresh tomatoes,
chopped spring onions, olive oil and
red wine vinegar (or use diced, fresh tomatoes
or sour cream) coriander (cilantro) leaves, to garnish

Wash the spinach leaves (don't dry them) then place in a microwave-proof bowl and cover with cling wrap. Cook in the microwave for a few minutes, stirring occasionally, until they are wilted. Squeeze out as much water as possible, then set aside for the time being. Heat some oil in a large frypan cook onion and garlic for a few minutes, or until the onion is translucent. Add corn, tomato paste, water and chilli. Cook over low heat for a minute or two then add cooked spinach. Stir to combine then allow to cool.

Place four tortillas on a flat surface. Spread a spoonful or two of refried beans over each tortilla, scatter some corn mixture over the top, then sprinkle with grated cheese. Top with the remaining four tortillas.

For a simple tomato salsa combine diced ripe tomato, chopped spring onions, a splash of good olive oil and some red wine vinegar.

Remove the quesadillas from their cling wrap. Heat a little olive oil in a large frypan and cook the quesadillas, one at a time. When they are lightly browned carefully turn them over and cook on the other side.

Serve by slicing tortillas in six and serve with salsa or sour cream, diced tomatoes and coriander leaves.

Quesadillas are great as a snack in small quantities or as a light meal with a side salad.

pita pizza

Serves 4 (1 pita bread per serve)

4 small wholegrain pita breads
½ cup (4 fl oz) commercial pasta sauce
3 large tomatoes, sliced
1 medium green capsicum, de-seeded and sliced
1 cup sliced mushrooms

1 medium onion, peeled and sliced
8 tablespoons grated, low-fat cheese
16 black olives, chopped (optional)
1 zucchini sliced (optional)

Preheat oven to 180°C (350°F).

Spread pita breads with sauce. Arrange the vegetables evenly over the top and sprinkle with grated cheese. Place on a baking tray.

Bake in oven for 15-20 minutes or until cheese melts and begins to brown.

Serve pita pizzas straight from the oven, accompanied by a tossed salad.

Storage: Wrap prepared but uncooked pizzas in plastic film or slide into big freezer bags and freeze until needed, then place the frozen pizzas on a baking tray and bake for 25 minutes.

The beauty of this recipe is that by using pita bread as the pizza base, you can put the whole dish together very quickly making it an ideal snack or light meal. The pizzas also freeze well.

potato gnocchi with four cheese sauce

Serves 6

FOUR CHEESE SAUCE
Makes 500ml (16fl oz)
50 g (1¾ oz) pecorini cheese
300 ml (10 fl oz) cream
200 g (6½ oz) good quality blue cheese
½ cup grated parmesan cheese
100 g (3½ oz) sharp cheddar, grated
2 tablespoons parsley

POTATO GNOCCHI
1 kg (2 lb) potatoes
200 g (6½ oz) plain flour
2 egg yolks
½ cup (4 oz) parmesan cheese
salt and pepper

In a small saucepan on low heat, place all ingredients for the sauce and heat just before boiling, whisking continuously until sauce reduces and all cheese has melted. Pass the sauce through a coarse sieve and serve with gnocchi immediately. To garnish, sprinkle with chopped parsley.

Boil potatoes in salted water until tender, approximately 20 minutes.

Drain, cool and peel then push through strainer or grater.

On a clean bench, spread out the flour, put the potato on top and add the yolks and cheese. Lightly knead the mix until it just comes together. Season well.

Divide into 3 pieces. Roll each piece out to 20 cm (8 in) thick lengths then cut into 2 cm (¾ in) gnocchi. Roll each with a fork to round off the edges. Use plenty of flour throughout this process. Toss small batches of the gnocchi in a colander to remove excess flour.

Drop batches of the gnocchi into rapidly boiling, well-salted water. As they rise to the surface, scoop out and toss in the prepared sauce (or refresh in ice water then drain, toss in oil and refrigerate for later. Plunge into boiling water for 2 minutes when ready to serve).

pan fried haloumi with asparagus and cherry tomatoes

Serves 6

2 punnets cherry tomatoes, on the vine if possible
100 ml (3 fl oz) olive oil
salt and cracked black pepper, to taste

2 bunches asparagus spears
360 g (12½ oz) haloumi, cut in triangle shape
2 lemons, juiced

Pre-heat oven to hot, 220°C (450°F).

Place tomatoes on a baking tray and brush with olive oil, salt and pepper and bake until skins blister, approximately 5–10 minutes. Be careful not to overcook.

Blanch asparagus in pot of boiling water for 1 minute and refresh in cold water to retain its vibrant green colour.

Arrange asparagus and cherry tomatoes on a plate.

Heat a non-stick fry pan on medium heat and fry haloumi for 30 seconds each side until golden brown. Add to dish and serve immediately while still warm with a squeeze of lemon and cracked black pepper to serve.

The unique squeaky texture and salty flavour of haloumi cheese is the hit in this dish. Try to source an authentic Greek style for the best flavour. As fabulous as haloumi is, make sure it is served still warm to fully appreciate its magic, or it becomes tough and loses its pizzazz!

frittata di zucchine

(Zucchini tart)
Serves 6

Olive oil	6 eggs
500 g (1 lb) medium sized zucchini (courgette), cut into thick rings	½ bunch continental parsley
salt and pepper, to taste	50 g (2 oz) parmesan cheese, grated

Place a small amount of oil in the pan, when hot add your zucchini, sauté stirring frequently, add salt and pepper.

When zucchini are soft and a rich golden in colour place them in a colander.

When cold, put zucchini in a bowl, add eggs, parsley and cheese. Mix together.

Now in the same frying pan add approximately 10 ml (⅓ fl oz) of oil and fry the mixed ingredients.

Cook over a moderate heat, not stirring contents of pan for one or two minutes, so that the bottom will set.

Finish cooking the frittata in a moderate oven, 180°C (350°F) for approximately 15 minutes or until the top becomes a lovely, dark, rich golden colour. Allow to cool.

When cold, run a spatula along the bottom and tip contents onto a round plate. This dish is generally served cold.

parmiggiana di melanzana

(Eggplant lasagna)
Serves 6

5 large eggplants (aubergines)	50 g (2 oz) parmesan cheese
vegetable oil	100 g (3½ oz) mozzarella cheese
plain flour	1 bunch fresh basil
300 g (9½ oz) peeled tomatoes, crushed	salt and pepper, to taste

Peel and cut eggplant into slices (lengthwise), ½ cm (¼ in) thick.

Salt the slices and leave them in a colander so that the water can drain (also to take any bitter taste out of them).

Pour oil into a heavy frying pan and let it heat up. Dust eggplant lightly on both sides with the fl our, then fry the eggplant, turning over to cook both sides, until they are golden brown.

Place fried eggplant on absorbent towel to drain. On a platter, spread a thin layer of salsa pomodoro, place an even layer of eggplant on top, then add second spread of sauce followed by sprinkled parmesan cheese. Randomly place thin slices of mozzarella and ripped fresh basil leaves over this.

Cover with another layer of eggplant and repeat process for 3 to 4 layers, to personal taste. Finish the dish with a spread of the sauce and parmesan cheese. Bake in a slow oven, 150°C (300°F) for 20 minutes.

fettuccine di spinaci alle verdure

(Spinach fettuccine with vegetables)
Serves 4

2 packets (600 g, 1¼ lb) spinach fettuccine
50 ml (2 fl oz) olive oil
2 cloves of garlic, sliced
6 medium button mushrooms, sliced
1 small zucchini (courgette), sliced

Salt and black pepper, to taste
1 punnet cherry tomatoes, halved
1 stem fresh basil leaves
50 ml (2 fl oz) extra virgin olive oil

Cook the fettuccine in 6 litres of boiling salted water to al dente stage (firm) stirring constantly.

While the pasta is cooking, heat the olive oil over high heat in a heavy pan large enough to fit the pasta. Add the garlic and sauté quickly. Add the mushrooms and zucchini and sauté for a couple of minutes. Season with salt and add the tomatoes. Cook until they just start to soften.

Add the basil leaves and the strained pasta with two tablespoons of water from the pasta. Pour over the extra virgin olive oil and stir through.

Serve finished with black pepper.

minestra di lenticchie

(Lentil soup)
Serves 4

60 ml (2 fl oz) olive oil
3 medium carrots
1 large leek
½ bunch small celery
4 slices flat pancetta (with fat on)
3 bay leaves
salt, to taste

4 litres (7 pints) water
200 g (6½ oz) brown lentils
3 tomatoes, de-seeded and chopped
½ bunch continental parsley, chopped
50 g (2 oz) parmesan cheese, grated
60 ml (2fl oz) extra virgin olive oil
pepper, to taste

Chop all the ingredients into small pieces.

In a heavy pot (or even a terracotta one) heat the olive oil and sauté the carrots, leek, celery and pancetta, together with the bay leaves for about 5 minutes stirring frequently over a moderate to high heat and don't forget to salt liberally.

Add the water and lentils at the same time and bring to the boil. After which turn the heat down to low for simmering.

Simmer for about 1 hour and then add the tomatoes, cooking for a further 30 minutes.

Place in a soup bowl, adding the parsley, parmesan and drizzle with the extra virgin olive oil. Add pepper to taste.

When served to your guests, prepare chargrilled crusty bread as an accompaniment.

thai pumpkin soup

Serves 6

2 litres (4¼ pints) water
1 kg (2 lbs) pumpkin, peeled and cut into chunks
1 medium potato
1 medium onion
1 vegetable stock cube
2 tablespoons chopped lemongrass

½ cup coriander, chopped
1 teaspoon ginger, chopped
½ cup coconut milk
salt, to taste
chilli powder, to taste

Place the water, pumpkin, potato, onion, and stock cube in a large pot and boil until the vegetables are soft.

Remove the vegetables with a slotted spoon and puree in a food processor, adding lemongrass, coriander and ginger. Return to the boiling pot and mix in the coconut milk. Add salt and chilli last and garnish with a sprig of parsley.

coconut korma

Serves 4

60 ml (2 fl oz) oil
125 g (4 oz) onion, sliced
2 cloves garlic, chopped
2½ cm (1 in) piece ginger, peeled and grated
3 cardamom pods, split
1 tablespoon curry paste
1 tablespoon tomato puree
400 g (13 oz) can chopped tomatoes
75 g (3 oz) red lentils
350 g (11 oz) tofu, cubed
500 g (1 lb) seasonal vegetables, chopped into bite-sized pieces

1 teaspoon ground coriander
1 teaspoon ground cinnamon
1 teaspoon ground cumin
1 teaspoon ground turmeric
salt and pepper, to taste
600 ml (20 fl oz) vegetable stock
150 ml (5 fl oz) coconut milk
2 tablespoons chopped fresh coriander
rice, to serve

Heat a tablespoon of the oil in a large deep frying pan. Fry onion, garlic, ginger and cardamom pods for 5 minutes. Add curry paste, tomato puree, tomatoes and lentils. Cook for further 10 minutes.

Heat the remaining oil in a separate pan and stir-fry tofu for 5 minutes. Add the vegetables and spices, season and cook for 10 minutes. Stir in the tomato and lentil mixture. Add stock, cover and simmer for 20 minutes or until lentils are almost cooked, stirring occasionally. Stir in the coconut milk and coriander, reserving a little for garnish. Cook uncovered for a further 10 minutes. Garnish with coriander and serve with rice.

tomato and herb soup

Serves 4

60 g (2 oz) butter	6 black peppercorns
1 tablespoon each finely chopped celery, onion and carrot	½ bay leaf
¼ clove garlic, crushed	1.25 litres (2 pints) beef stock
2 tablespoons plain flour	500 g (1 lb) tomatoes, skinned and chopped
1 teaspoon dried mixed herbs	3 cloves
	salt and freshly ground black pepper, to taste

Melt butter in a large saucepan, add celery, onion, carrot and garlic and sauté, covered, over a medium heat, for 5 minutes. Stir in flour. Add mixed herbs, peppercorns, and bay leaf, then cover and cook gently for a further 5 minutes. Add stock, tomatoes and cloves. Cover and simmer gently for 1 hour. Add salt and pepper and serve.

Variations: Add ½ cup (4 oz) cooked rice, or 30 g (1 oz) tomato paste or ½ cup (4 oz) cooked, chopped ham, during last 10 minutes. For a creamy tomato soup stir in 150 ml (5 fl oz) of cream before serving.

SPECIALS

Ant ̶asto Melt

Chi̶ ̶n Bliss ̶ ̶ie-w̲
̶akin, spina̶ ̶ayo & che̶

̶ato,
̶ lettuce

salads
and sides

caesar salad with garlic croutons

Serves 6-8

1 clove garlic, peeled and cut in half
1 cos (Romaine) lettuce, leaves washed and dried
1 teaspoon salt
1 endive, leaves washed and dried
1 teaspoon dry mustard (see glossary)
2 tablespoons Parmesan cheese, shaved
1 tablespoon lemon juice
4 anchovy fillets, chopped into 3-4 pieces
¼ teaspoon Tabasco sauce
1 coddled egg (boiled for 1 minute)
3 tablespoons olive oil

CROUTONS
4 slices whitebread
2 cloves garlic, crushed
salt
olive oil, for frying

Rub wooden salad bowl with cut clove of garlic. Put salt, mustard, lemon juice and Tabasco sauce into bowl and stir with wooden spoon until salt dissolves. Add olive oil and blend well.

Tear salad greens into bite-sized pieces and place in salad bowl. Sprinkle with shaved Parmesan and add anchovy fillets. Break in the coddled egg and toss well, until all ingredients are well coated with dressing.

To make croutons, remove crusts from bread and cut slices into 1 cm (½ in) cubes. Fry cubes in hot oil with garlic until golden. Drain well, and sprinkle with salt before serving.

Just before serving salad, sprinkle with croutons and toss again.

calamari salad with basil dressing

Serves 2

300 g (10 oz) calamari tubes,
washed and sliced into 1 cm (½ in) rings
1 cup (8 fl oz) of simmering water in saucepan
⅓ cup (2¾ fl oz) lemon juice
⅓ cup (2¾ fl oz) grapeseed oil (see glossary)
150 g (5 oz) snow peas, trimmed
100 g (3½ oz) button mushrooms
1 punnet cherry tomatoes
1 green capsicum (bell pepper),
seeds and pith removed and cut into strips
2 tablespoons chives, chopped
½ cup fresh basil, chopped

FRENCH DRESSING
3 parts oil
1 part balsamic vinegar
salt and freshly ground black pepper, to taste

Cook calamari in simmering water for two minutes or until cooked. Drain.

In a bowl, combine lemon juice and grapeseed oil, then add calamari. Toss calamari until coated. Cover bowl with cling wrap and refrigerate overnight.

Place snow peas, mushrooms, tomatoes, capsicum and chives into a salad bowl.

Drain calamari, reserving marinade. Add calamari to salad bowl and chill for 30 minutes, covered.

In a bowl or jar, combine french dressing ingredients, add basil and reserved marinade. Chill for 30 minutes.

Just before serving, drizzle basil dressing over salad and toss lightly.

coleslaw

Serves 4–6

½ small cabbage, shredded	MAYONNAISE
2 carrots, grated	2 egg yolks
1 onion, grated	1 teaspoon white wine vinegar
1 clove garlic, crushed (optional)	½ teaspoon salt
1 stalk celery, thinly sliced	½ teaspoon dry mustard (see glossary)
	pinch of white pepper
	⅔ cup (5 fl oz) olive oil
	few drops of lemon juice

First make the mayonnaise. Make sure your bowl is well washed and dried. Beat egg yolks, vinegar, salt, dry mustard and pepper with an egg beater or an electric beater set at medium speed. Add olive oil, drop by drop, whisking continuously, until about two tablespoons have been added. Add a few drops of lemon juice, to bring mixture to the consistency of cream. Add remaining oil in a thin steady stream, beating continuously, stopping the addition of the oil from time to time to make sure the mixture is combining well. When all the oil has been added and the mayonnaise is thick, add extra lemon juice to taste. Adjust seasoning.

Mix cabbage, carrots, onion, garlic and celery in a large salad bowl. Stir mayonnaise through the salad and serve immediately.

Note: If the mayonnaise curdles, wash the beater, beat one egg yolk in another bowl and very slowly add the curdled mayonnaise to the fresh egg yolk, beating continuously.

crab salad

Serves 4

400 g (12 oz) crabmeat, freshly cooked or canned
4 crisp celery sticks, finely chopped
½ cup (4 fl oz) French dressing
salt and freshly ground black pepper, to taste

4 crisp lettuce leaves, to serve
2 hard-boiled eggs, sliced to garnish
4 sprigs parsley, to garnish

In a mixing bowl, combine crabmeat and celery. Moisten with French dressing and salt and pepper and mix well. Pile into small salad bowls lined with crisp lettuce leaves. Garnish with slices of hard-boiled egg and parsley and serve.

creamy mashed potatoes

Serves 4

4 medium-sized potatoes, peeled
½ cup (4 fl oz) milk
30 g (1 oz) butter

60 g (2 oz) tasty cheese, grated
salt and freshly ground black pepper, to taste

Place potatoes into a saucepan with cold, lightly salted water to cover. Bring to the boil and cook gently, covered, for 20–30 minutes, until potatoes are easily pierced with a fork. Drain thoroughly, then shake pan over heat for a minute or two until all surplus moisture has evaporated and potatoes are quite dry.

Mash potatoes, then beat with a wooden spoon until very smooth. In a saucepan, heat milk and butter. Once mixture is hot, add to potatoes and beat until light and fluffy. Add cheese and stir through until melted. Season with salt and pepper and serve immediately.

garlic bread

Serves 4

1 baguette | 250 g (8 oz) butter, room temperature
4 cloves garlic, peeled and crushed | 2 tablespoon fresh parsley, finely chopped

Preheat oven to 220°C (420°F). With a sharp knife, cut bread into slices almost to the bottom of the loaf, being careful not to cut right through.

In a small bowl, mash garlic thoroughly into butter, then stir through parsley. Spread garlic butter generously on both sides of bread slices. Wrap bread loosely in aluminium foil, place in the oven for 10–15 minutes, or until bread is crisp and golden. Serve hot.

lobster salad

Serves 4

2 medium-sized lobsters, cooked | 2 lemons, sliced
4 iceberg lettuce cups | 2 tomatoes, sliced
⅔ cup (5 oz) mayonnaise | ½ cucumber, sliced

Crack lobster claws with a lobster cracker or a light weight of some sort and remove meat. Carefully remove meat from the shells with a fine skewer. Dice meat and place back in the shells. Arrange lobster in lettuce cups, and top with mayonnaise, lemon, tomatoes and cucumber.

pasta salad

Serves 6-8

500 g (1 lb) cooked spiral noodles
1 tablespoon olive oil
½ teaspoon salt
½ red capsicum (bell pepper),
seeds and pith removed and diced

4-6 mushrooms, sliced
4-6 shallots, finely chopped
125 g (4 oz) corn kernels (optional)
125 g (4 oz) mung bean sprouts
300 ml (10 fl oz) bottle of coleslaw dressing

Place pasta into a large saucepan of boiling water with oil and salt, and cook for eight minutes or until pasta is al dente. Rinse, strain and allow to cool.

Place all ingredients except dressing in a bowl and toss to combine. Add dressing to taste.

potato croquettes

Serves 6

500 g (1 lb) potatoes, peeled
30 g (1 oz) butter
1 egg yolk
2 tablespoons hot milk
salt and freshly ground black pepper, to taste

seasoned flour (see glossary)
2 eggs, beaten
breadcrumbs for coating
olive oil for frying

Cook potatoes in boiling salted water until tender. Drain, then dry potatoes with a clean tea towel. Mash and press through a sieve or potato ricer. Return to pan. Add butter, egg yolk, milk, and salt and pepper, and beat until smooth. Divide mixture into small pieces similar to the shape of wine corks.

Roll croquettes in seasoned flour, then brush with egg and roll in breadcrumbs. Deep fry in hot oil until golden brown.

potato salad

Serves 6–8

1 kg (2 lb) waxy potatoes, peeled
⅓ cup (2¾ fl oz) French dressing
½ cup cucumber, finely chopped
½ cup celery, finely chopped
¼ cup onion, finely sliced
4 hard-boiled eggs, coarsely chopped

1 cup (8 oz) mayonnaise
½ cup (4 fl oz) sour cream
1 tablespoon horseradish relish
salt and freshly ground black pepper, to taste
2 rashers bacon, cooked and finely chopped,
to garnish

Cook potatoes in boiling salted water until just tender. Drain well and leave to cool just enough to be handled, then cut into cubes.

Place diced potatoes in a bowl and pour over French dressing while potatoes are still warm. Let potatoes cool, then add cucumber, celery, onion and egg.

In a separate bowl, combine mayonnaise, sour cream and horseradish relish. Pour over potatoes and toss gently. Season with salt and pepper.

Garnish with bacon just before serving.

tabouleh with avocado dressing

Serves 6

⅔ cup (5½ oz) cracked wheat (see glossary)
hot water, to cover cracked wheat
2 tomatoes, finely chopped
1 zucchini (courgette), finely chopped
1 cup celery, finely chopped
1½ cups flat-leaf parsley, chopped
1 level tablespoon mint, chopped
¼ cup chives, chopped
1 teaspoon dill, finely chopped, to garnish
1 cup cashews, chopped, to garnish

AVOCADO DRESSING
1 avocado, peeled and chopped
2 teaspoons lemon juice
3 teaspoons tarragon vinegar (see glossary)
1 teaspoon grapeseed oil (see glossary)
1 tablespoon water
pinch of lemon pepper
pinch of salt
6 drops Tabasco sauce

In a large bowl, cover cracked wheat with hot water and leave to soak for 15 minutes. Drain well, squeezing out excess liquid. Add tomatoes, zucchini, celery, parsley, mint and chives to cracked wheat. Mix well, then chill.

To make avocado dressing, place all ingredients in a blender or food processor and blend until smooth. Add more oil of required. Chill well.

To serve, pour dressing over salad and toss lightly, then sprinkle with dill and cashews.

thai beef salad

Serves 6

	DRESSING
6 large lettuce leaves	4 kaffir lime leaves, cut into strips
500 g (1 lb) beef rump or tenderloin, roasted and sliced into strips	3 cloves garlic, finely chopped
2 cloves garlic, finely chopped	5 green serrano chillies, seeded and finely chopped
1 red onion, sliced	1 tablespoon fish sauce
grated lemon zest, to taste	juice of 1 lime
¼ cup coriander (cilantro) leaves, torn	¼ cup palm sugar or brown sugar
1 cup mint leaves, torn	
fried onion, to garnish	
1 tablespoon dried chilli flakes, to garnish	

To make the salad dressing, combine all ingredients in a bowl (or jar) and mix well (or put lid on and shake).

To serve, arrange lettuce leaves on a serving dish, covering the whole surface area. Place strips of beef over lettuce and sprinkle over garlic, onion, lemongrass, coriander and mint.

Pour the dressing over the top and garnish with fried onion and chilli flakes.

tuna salad

Serves 4

1 x 425 g (15 oz) can tuna in brine
1 large dill pickle, chopped (see glossary)
4 spring onions (scallions), sliced
1 cup peas, cooked
1 red capsicum (bell pepper),
seeds and pith removed and sliced

¼ cup (1 oz) walnuts, coarsely broken
salt and freshly ground black pepper, to taste
¼ cup (2 oz) sour cream
4 iceberg lettuce cups, for serving
2 eggs, hard-boiled and finely chopped,
to garnish

In a bowl, break tuna into large chunks and toss with dill pickle, spring onions, peas, red capsicum, walnuts and salt and pepper. Add sour cream and mix through gently.

Spoon into lettuce cups and sprinkle with chopped egg before serving.

waldorf salad

Serves 6

1 green apple
1 red apple
juice of ½ lemon
1 cup celery, finely chopped

½ cup walnuts, chopped
½ cup (2 oz) mayonnaise
6 crisp iceberg lettuce cups
1 red apple, thinly sliced, brushed with
lemon juice to prevent discolouration, to garnish

Chill apples, then core and dice them. Pour lemon juice over apples. Add celery, walnuts and mayonnaise and combine.

Serve piled into lettuce cups and garnish with slices of red apple.

lamb salad

Serves 4-6

¾ cup cracked wheat	250 g (8 oz) cooked lamb, diced
185 ml (6¼ fl oz) hot water	1 onion, finely chopped
1 teaspoon butter	½ cup celery, sliced
½ teaspoon ground tarragon	2 tablespoons natural yoghurt
1 chicken stock cube, crumbled	2 tablespoons mayonnaise
½ teaspoon curry powder	lettuce cups, for serving
1½ teaspoons dry mustard (see glossary)	2 hard-boiled eggs, sliced, to garnish
½ teaspoon cayenne pepper	parsley sprigs, to garnish

Combine wheat, water, butter, ground tarragon, stock cube, curry powder, dry mustard and cayenne in a saucepan and heat, stirring, until the mixture boils.

Reduce heat, cover, and simmer for 10 minutes, or until all liquid is absorbed. Cool.

Add lamb, onion, celery, yoghurt and mayonnaise, and toss well. Chill for 30 minutes before serving.

To serve, spoon salad into lettuce cups, and garnish with egg slices and parsley.

salad with crispy noodles and sugar

Serves 4

1 cabbage, finely chopped	1 small packet crispy noodles
1 onion, diced	small tin dried tomato tuna
2 carrots, grated	1 tablespoon balsamic
2 tablespoons cheese, grated	1 tablespoon Thousand Island dressing

Combine cabbage, onion and carrots in a bowl. Add cheese, noodles and tomato tuna. Drizzle Balsamic and Thousand Island Dressing across the salad and toss.

classic greek salad

Serves 4

4 Roma tomatoes	14 kalamata olives
1 cucumber	1 teaspoon dried mountain oregano
½ red onion	1 teaspoon sea salt flakes
½ turnip	40 ml (1½ fl oz) olive oil
3 tablespoons Dodoni feta	red kahel, to garnish

Remove the core from the tomatoes and roughly chop.

Peel and deseed the cucumber and roughly chop.

Using a mandolin, finely slice the onion and turnip into rings.

In a large bowl, mix together the tomato, cucmber, onion, feta, olives and turnip. Season with the oregano and salt. Drissle with the oil. Check seasonings and serve with red kahel to garnish.

This is a classic Greek salad and notice one thing: it doesn't mention any lettuce. Why not? Because a genuine greek salad doesn't contain any lettuce.

pollo all'insalata

(Chicken salad)
Serves 4

olive oil
2 Spanish onions, sliced
50 g (2 oz) pine nuts
400 g (13 oz) breast of chicken,
skin off and cut into strips

salt and pepper, to taste
60 ml (2 fl oz) chicken stock
60 ml (2 fl oz) balsamic vinegar
Mesculin or mixed lettuce

Heat the oil in a shallow pan, add the sliced onions, season and then sauté for a few minutes.

Add the pine nuts, stir frequently without toasting them, then add the strips of chicken, salt, pepper and cook till golden brown.

Deglaze the pan with the stock, keep the heat on high and lastly add the balsamic vinegar. Reduce all the juices and toss the pan to amalgamate all the flavours.

Place the lettuce on a plate and top with the chicken pieces then evenly spread the rest of the ingredients over the top. Don't forget to include the cooking juices in the dish, you can mop them up with bread. Finish with a generous amount of freshly crushed pepper and WOW!

roast pumpkin and couscous salad

Serves 4

1 kg (2 lbs) pumpkin	fresh red chilli, chopped
oil spray	2 tablespoons ground cumin
freshly ground black pepper	¾ tablespoon ground cinnamon
1½ cups couscous	¾ cup macadamia nuts, roughly chopped
boiling water	¾ cup pitted dried dates, quartered
1 tablespoon oil	rocket leaves
large red onion, chopped	175 g (5¾ oz) tub plain soy yoghurt

Cut pumpkin into small pieces, spray with oil and, sprinkle with ground black pepper and roast in a moderately hot oven, 200°C (400°F) until a skewer slips easily into flesh.

In a large heatproof bowl add 1½ cups (12 fl oz) of boiling water to the couscous and let it be absorbed. Heat oil and cook the onion and chilli for approximately 1 minute. Add the cumin and cinnamon and cook for another minute, then add the macadamia nuts and dates. Stir the above through the couscous.

Arrange rocket leaves on a plate, sprinkle the pumpkin over, then the couscous and finally add natural soy yoghurt and serve.

warm chicken salad with quinoa

Serves 4-6

CHICKEN	SALAD
1 tablespoon olive oil	1 cup quinoa
400 g (13 oz) chicken breasts, cut into thick strips	2 cups water
1 teaspoon dried marjoram	¼ cup red onion, chopped
salt and pepper to taste	½ cup red capsicum, diced
	½ cup green capsicum, diced
	½ cup chopped fresh basil
	1 cup chopped tomato
	1 teaspoon garlic, crushed
	2 tablespoons apple cider vinegar
	3 tablespoons extra virgin olive oil
	1 teaspoon fresh chili

Mix all the chicken ingredients together in a bowl to coat chicken. Heat olive oil in a saucepan and cook chicken until golden brown.

Cook the quinoa in a saucepan with the two cups of water: Stir constantly over medium heat about 5 minutes till it just becomes aromatic.

Reduce the heat to low, cover the pan and simmer for about 15 minutes. Drain the quinoa if necessary and then transfer it to a large bowl.

Add all the remaining ingredients including the chicken and thoroughly combine with the quinoa.

Add salt and pepper to taste and serve immediately.

tofu lettuce burgers

Serves 4

1 onion, finely chopped
1 garlic clove, crushed
2 tablespoons olive oil
1 cup hard tofu, crumbled
1-2 cups of wholemeal breadcrumbs
2 eqggs, cracked
½ cup carrot, finely grated

2 tablespoons Worcestershire sauce
½ teaspoon sea salt
1 teaspoon pepper
4 large cos (Romaine) lettuce leaves, washed and dried
1 tomato, sliced

Sauté the garlic and onion in a frying pan in 1 tablespoon of olive oil until a light golden brown.

Place the onion mixture into a mixing bowl and then add all the remaining ingredients apart from the lettuce and tomato, and mix thoroughly.

Shape the mixture into 4 burgers.

Heat the remaining olive oil in the frying pan.

Place the tofu burgers into the frying pan and cook for 4-5 minutes on each side.

Serve the burgers in the lettuce with a little tomato.

pasta, noodles and rice

cannelloni stuffed with ricotta in tomato sauce

Serves 4-6

12 cannelloni tubes	pinch of ground nutmeg
375 g (12 oz) ricotta cheese	4-6 large ripe tomatoes, skinned and chopped
2 eggs	3 tablespoons olive oil
60 g (2 oz) Parmesan cheese	60 g (2 oz) butter
salt and freshly ground black pepper, to taste	

Preheat oven to 180°C (350°F). Cook cannelloni tubes according to packet instructions. Drain and set aside until ready to fill.

In a bowl, mix ricotta cheese, eggs and half the Parmesan thoroughly. Season with salt, pepper and nutmeg.

Place tomatoes in a saucepan and cook, uncovered, until they are a thick pulp, stirring occasionally. Remove from heat and stir in oil gradually.

Drain cannelloni and fill with ricotta cheese mixture. Place filled cannelloni side by side in a single layer in a buttered shallow baking dish. Pour tomato sauce around and over the cannelloni, sprinkle with remaining parmesan cheese and dot with butter. Bake in the oven for 20 minutes or until sauce is bubbling. Serve immediately.

fettucine alfredo

Serves 4

250 g (8 oz) fettuccine
125 g (4 oz) butter
125 g (4 oz) Parmesan cheese, grated
¼ teaspoon salt

freshly ground black pepper, to taste
1 cup (8 fl oz) fresh cream
parsley, finely chopped, to granish
extra Parmesan cheese, to garnish

Cook fettucine for 15 minutes, or until al dente, in a large saucepan of rapidly boiling, salted water.

Meanwhile, melt butter in a large saucepan, then add Parmesan, salt, pepper and cream. Cook over a low heat, stirring constantly, until blended.

Drain fettucine. Immediately add to cheese mixture and toss until pasta is well coated. Place in a heated serving dish, sprinkle with parsley and extra Parmesan and serve immediately.

fettucine carbonara

Serves 4

250-375 g (8-12 oz) fettucine
2 tablespoons olive oil
3 slices bacon, rind removed and finely diced
2 eggs

45 g (1½ oz) Parmesan cheese, grated
1 cup (8 fl oz) fresh cream
freshly ground black pepper, to taste

Cook fettucine for 15 minutes, or until al dente, in a large saucepan of rapidly boiling, salted water.

Just before fettucine is ready, heat oil and fry bacon.

In a bowl, beat eggs and add cheese.

Drain pasta and return to the hot saucepan. Add cheese and egg mixture, cream, plenty of black pepper and the crisp bacon. Mix well. Place the saucepan over a low heat for a minute or so, stirring constantly until heated through.

Place in a hot dish and serve immediately.

gnocchi

Serves 4

	ITALIAN TOMATO SAUCE
3 medium-sized potatoes, washed	2 tablespoons olive oil
125 g (4 oz) plain (all-purpose) flour, sifted	1 small onion, finely chopped
1 egg	2 cloves garlic, crushed
1½ teaspoons salt	1 kg (2 lb) tomatoes, skinned, seeded and chopped
extra plain (all-purpose) flour	or 2 x 400 g (13 oz) cans whole tomatoes, diced
parmesan cheese, grated, to garnish	½ teaspoon salt
	½ teaspoon caster (superfine) sugar, or to taste
	¼ teaspoon freshly ground black pepper
	2 leaves basil
	1 sprig oregano
	1 bay leaf
	1 tablespoon tomato paste

First, make the Italian tomato sauce. In a large saucepan, heat oil. Add onion and garlic and cook for about six minutes, stirring, until onion is translucent. Add tomatoes and all other ingredients and bring to the boil. Reduce heat, cover, and simmer for 45 minutes, stirring occasionally. Purée sauce in a blender or food processor if you want a smooth consistency.

To make the gnocchi, boil unpeeled potatoes until tender. Peel while hot and place in a mixing bowl. Mash potatoes straight away, adding sifted flour, a little at a time, while potatoes are still hot. Add egg and salt and beat until smooth.

Turn potato mixture onto a well-floured board and knead, working in enough flour to form a smooth, soft, non-sticky dough. Divide dough into several parts. Roll each to pencil thickness. Cut into 2 cm (¾ in) pieces. With the tines of a floured fork, press each piece so that it curls. Place on waxed paper. Sprinkle lightly with flour. Cook immediately, or within two hours.

Add gnocchi a little at a time to a large pot of rapidly boiling salted water with a little oil added. Cook for about five minutes, or until gnocchi comes to the surface. Drain and keep warm in a heated bowl until all gnocchi is cooked.

Serve with Italian tomato sauce, sprinkled with Parmesan cheese.

italian marinara

Serves 6–8

MARINARA MIX	
1 kg (2 lb) marinara mix (oysters, scallops, prawns/shrimp, crayfish, all shelled) and fish fillet pieces	¼ cup (2 fl oz) olive oil
	1 teaspoon oregano
	¼ teaspoon freshly ground black pepper
	2 tablespoons red wine (optional)
	1 teaspoon parsley, chopped
375 g (12 oz) spaghetti	2 cloves garlic, sliced
salt to taste	2 x 400 g (13 oz) cans tomatoes, puréed

Wash and drain marinara mix. Heat oil in a large frying pan and sauté marinara mix over a medium heat for five minutes. Set pan aside and keep warm. Add garlic to another pan and sauté until golden. Stir in tomatoes, salt, oregano, parsley, pepper and wine (if using). Cook rapidly, uncovered, for 15 minutes, or until sauce has thickened. Stir occasionally. If sauce becomes too thick, add ¼–½ cup (2–4 fl oz) water. Add marinara mix and reheat gently.

Meanwhile, cook spaghetti for 15 minutes or until al dente in boiling, salted water and drain. Serve immediately with marinara sauce poured on top.

lasagne

Serves 4-6

2 tablespoons olive oil	2 cups (16 fl oz) water
250 g (8 oz) minced (ground) beef	½ teaspoon salt
250 g (8 oz) lean pork, minced	½ teaspoon freshly ground black pepper
1 onion, finely chopped	250 g (8 oz) lasagne sheets
1 clove garlic, finely chopped	30 g (1 oz) mozzarella cheese, sliced thinly
1 teaspoon parsley, chopped	250 g (8 oz) ricotta cheese, crumbed
250 g (8 oz) tomato paste	2 tablespoons Romano cheese, grated
	1½ teaspoon salt

Heat oil in a large saucepan, add beef and pork and brown with onion, garlic and parsley. Stir in tomato paste, water, ½ teaspoon salt, and pepper and simmer, uncovered, for 1½ hours.

Preheat oven to 180°C (350°F). Bring a large pot of water to the boil, add 1½ teaspoons salt and the lasagne sheets. Boil for 20 minutes or until al dente, stirring constantly but very gently to prevent lasagne sheets sticking. Drain.

Wipe a little oil over the base of a large shallow rectangular baking dish, and arrange alternate layers of lasagne sheets, sauce, mozzarella and ricotta cheese. Repeat layers until lasagne sheets and sauce and two cheeses are all used, ending with ricotta cheese. Sprinkle with grated Romano cheese and bake in the oven for 25-30 minutes. Allow to stand for 10 minutes before serving.

mushroom and onion risotto

Serves 4

30 g (1 oz) butter
1 small onion, chopped or sliced
1 rasher bacon, rind removed and diced
12 button mushrooms, sliced
300 g (10 oz) arborio rice

3 cups (24 fl oz) chicken stock, boiling
125 g (4 oz) tasty cheese, grated
2 tablespoons fresh parsley, finely chopped
salt and freshly ground black pepper, to taste

Melt butter in a heavy-based saucepan, and fry onion, bacon and mushrooms, stirring once or twice, for about four minutes. Stir in rice and cook for about two minutes.

Pour in ½ cup of hot stock, stirring constantly until liquid is absorbed. Continue stirring while adding each ½ cup of stock until all liquid is absorbed each time. Cook rice for 30 minutes or until tender. Add extra hot water or stock if necessary. Stir through cheese and parsley. Season with salt and pepper. Serve with a green salad.

prawn risotto

Serves 4

4 tablespoons olive oil
2 small onions, finely chopped
250 g (8 oz) arborio rice
¾ cup (6 fl oz) dry white wine
1 L (32 fl oz) fish stock

1 medium size onion, grated
500 g (1 lb) green prawns (shrimp), shelled
squeeze of lemon juice
chopped parsley and zest of 1 lemon, to garnish

Place two tablespoons oil in a frying pan and lightly brown onions. Add rice and cook, stirring constantly, until lightly browned. Add wine. When wine has evaporated, add stock gradually, a cup at a time. Allow rice to absorb the liquid before adding more stock. Stir lightly and simmer gently, uncovered, until rice is cooked. Add a little hot water or more wine if rice gets too dry.

Meanwhile, heat remaining oil in a saucepan and add grated onion, lemon juice and prawns. Fry lightly until onion is translucent and prawns are cooked – approximately five minutes. Stir through rice and serve sprinkled with parsley and lemon zest.

ravioli

Serves 6

PASTA DOUGH	FILLING
1 tablespoon salt	2 tablespoons olive oil
3 tablespoons olive oil	375 g (12 oz) minced (ground) beef
5 eggs, beaten	or shredded chicken
375 g (12 oz) plain (all-purpose) flour	250 g (8 oz) fresh spinach, cooked
	2 eggs, beaten
	1 tablespoon Parmesan cheese
	¾ teaspoon salt
	¼ teaspoon freshly ground black pepper
	1 quantity Italian tomato sauce
	grated Parmesan or Romano cheese, to garnish

First make the pasta dough. Combine salt, olive oil, and five eggs in a food processor. Gradually add flour, pulsing to mix. The dough is ready when it clings together and feels springy.

To make the filling, heat oil in a frying pan. Add meat and cook until browned, then set aside in a bowl. Finely chop spinach and mix with meat. Add eggs, Parmesan cheese, salt and pepper. Mix well. Set aside until ready to use.

Divide pasta dough into quarters. Roll each quarter until it is 3 mm (⅛ in) thick, and a rectangular shape. Cut dough lengthways (using a pastry cutter, if you have one) into strips 12 cm (5 in) wide. Place two teaspoons of filling in the centre of one half of the pastry every 8.5 cm (3½ in), then fold over the other half, covering the filling. Seal the whole strip by pressing the long edges together with the tines of a fork. Press the two layers of pastry together between the mounds of filling and cut in the middle between mounds with the pastry cutter, again sealing the cut edges with the tines of a fork.

Add ravioli gradually, about a third at a time, to a large saucepan of rapidly boiling, salted water. Cook for 20 minutes or until tender. Remove with a slotted spoon. Drain well.

Serve topped with heated Italian tomato sauce and sprinkled with Parmesan or Romano cheese.

seafood risotto

Serves 6

½ cup (4 fl oz) olive oil
1 medium onion, chopped
2 cloves garlic, chopped
660 g (1 lb 5 oz) arborio rice
1 bunch shallots (green onions), chopped
1 bunch fresh coriander (cilantro), chopped
1 medium pumpkin, chopped into small chunks

1.5 L (48 fl oz) fish stock
1 cup (8 fl oz) dry white wine
1 kg (2 lb) marinara mix (see page 69)
¾ cup (3 oz) parmesan cheese, grated
salt and freshly ground black pepper, to taste
3 tablespoons sour cream

Wash and dry marinara mix and set aside.

Heat oil in a large saucepan and gently fry onion and garlic. When onion is translucent, add rice. Stir well, until rice is coated with oil. Add shallots and coriander and cook for a few minutes, then add pumpkin.

Add 1 cup (8 fl oz) stock, stirring constantly until liquid is absorbed into the rice. Add wine and continue to stir. Continue to add stock by the cupful and stir regularly, until all stock is absorbed. It will take about 30 minutes to get the rice to an almost cooked stage.

When rice is almost cooked, fold in the marinara mix and cook for a further five minutes. Add some of the Parmesan. Season with salt and pepper. Cook for another few minutes, until seafood is done, then stir in sour cream.

Serve in bowls, and sprinkle the last of the Parmesan on top.

spaghetti bolognaise

Serves 4

1 tablespoon olive oil	freshly ground black pepper, to taste
250 g (8 oz) minced (ground) beef	pinch of sugar
1 clove garlic, crushed	3 tablespoons tomato paste
1 large onion, finely grated	1 cup (8 fl oz) beef stock
500 g (1 lb) peeled tomatoes, chopped	250 g (8 oz) spaghetti
1 teaspoon oregano or basil	Parmesan cheese, to garnish
1 teaspoon salt	

Heat oil in frying pan, add meat, garlic and onion and brown lightly. Add tomatoes, oregano, salt, pepper and sugar.

In a small bowl, blend tomato paste with stock. Add this to mixture in frying pan. Simmer for 30 minutes, uncovered, so that sauce thickens slightly. Add water if needed to stop the bolognaise from drying out.

While sauce is cooking, cook spaghetti in boiling salted water until al dente (about 15 minutes). Drain spaghetti, and place on a hot serving dish or plate. Pour hot sauce over spaghetti and sprinkle with Parmesan cheese. Serve additional cheese in a small bowl.

spaghetti with meatballs

Serves 4-6

TOMATO SAUCE

1 x 400 g (13 oz) can whole tomatoes
1 cup (8 fl oz) Italian tomato sauce (see page 68)
125 g (4 oz) tomato paste
¼ cup (2 fl oz) water
¼ cup (2 fl oz) red wine
2 bay leaves, crushed
2 tablespoons parsley, chopped
1 clove garlic, crushed

MEATBALLS

4 slices white bread
500 g (1 lb) minced (ground) beef
1 tablespoon Parmesan cheese, grated
1 tablespoon parsley, chopped
1 tablespoon onion, grated
2 teaspoons salt
¼ teaspoon black pepper
¼ teaspoon oregano
1 egg, beaten
3 tablespoons olive oil
250 g (8 oz) spaghetti or thin spaghetti
Parmesan cheese, freshly grated, to garnish

To make tomato sauce, combine all ingredients in a large saucepan. Simmer until thick, stirring occasionally for about 10 minutes.

To make meatballs, place bread in a small bowl, add enough water to cover, and let stand for two minutes. Remove bread and squeeze out excess water. In a large bowl, combine bread with minced steak, Parmesan cheese, parsley, onion, salt, pepper, oregano and egg. Mix lightly until thoroughly combined. Shape into small balls. Heat oil in a frying pan and brown meatballs on all sides.

Add meatballs to sauce and simmer for 15-20 minutes. Meanwhile, cook spaghetti in salted, boiling water until al dente (about 15 minutes). Drain spaghetti and place on a hot serving dish or plate. Top with meatballs and sauce and sprinkle with Parmesan cheese.

springtime spaghetti

Serves 6-8

4-6 tomatoes, skinned and chopped
250 g (8 oz) cooked hot spaghetti, drained
1 green capsicum, chopped
½ cup spring onions, chopped
¼ cup black olives, chopped

salt and freshly ground black pepper, to taste
juice of half a lemon
80 ml (2¾ fl oz) olive oil
chopped parsley, to garnish
Parmesan cheese (optional)

Put tomatoes into a saucepan and heat, stirring. When they are hot, add spaghetti, capsicum, spring onions, olives, salt and pepper, lemon juice, and enough olive oil to coat pasta. Toss well.

Sprinkle with parsley and Parmesan cheese (if using) and serve immediately.

moussaka

Serves 6

4 tablespoons olive oil	2 tablespoons tomato paste
2 onions, finely chopped	150 ml (5 fl oz) beef stock
2 cloves garlic, crushed	2 medium eggplants, cut into 1 cm (½ in) slices
500 g (1 lb) lamb forequarter, chopped or minced	125 g (4 oz) plain flour
185 g (6 oz) mushrooms, chopped	salt and pepper, to taste
500 g (1 lb) tomatoes, skinned, seeded and chopped	90 g (3 oz) Parmesan cheese, grated
	1 tablespoon parsley, chopped

Preheat oven to 200°C (400°F). Heat 1 tablespoon olive oil in a large saucepan till hot, then sauté onion and garlic until soft, but not coloured. Add lamb and fry until lightly browned. Add mushrooms and tomatoes and cook for 5 minutes.

Add tomato paste and stock. Cook for a further 5 minutes.

Roll eggplant slices in flour. Heat remaining oil in a frying pan, and fry eggplant slices on both sides. Drain on absorbent paper. Line the base of an ovenproof casserole dish with slices of eggplant. Pour over some of the lamb mixture, season with salt and pepper and sprinkle with parsley. Cover with another layer of eggplant and repeat the process until casserole dish is full, finishing with a layer of eggplant. Sprinkle with Parmesan cheese and cook in the oven until golden brown—approximately 10–15 minutes. Serve sprinkled with chopped parsley.

Variation: Before adding the parmesan cheese, pour over a layer of béchamel sauce and cook in the oven for approximately 15–20 minutes.

mediterranean chicken pasta salad

Serves 6–8

6 chicken thighs 1.5kg (3 lb)	2 tablespoons Balsamic vinegar
chicken stock	3 cups pasta twirls
100 g (3½ oz) pesto	¼ stick of celery, sliced
200 g (6½ oz) sun-dried tomatoes in oil	salt and pepper to taste
200 g (6½ oz) snowpeas, blanched and sliced.	1 boutique lettuce, washed, drained and broken up.
10 small mushrooms	

Boil the chicken, cool then de-bone and cut up into small pieces manageable with a spoon.

Boil the pasta in chicken stock, then rinse in cold water and drain. When luke-warm, stir in the pesto and the sliced sundried tomatoes.

While you blanch the snow peas, slice the mushrooms and stir into the pasta. Drain the snow peas, slice, then add to the pasta mix with the celery.

(Variety can be achieved by different types of succulent leaves, the 'boutique' lettuce's have different colours, shapes and tastes. Capsicum, salad rocket or other mild herbs will work, but try to avoid strong flavours that will overpower such as onions, eschalots etc).

Finally add the chicken and sprinkle on the Balsamic vinegar and stir in. Let the dish sit for a few hours if possible.

When serving begin with a layer of leaves and top with the chicken

chinese egg noodle salad with chicken

Serves 6-8

1 double breast of chicken, thinly sliced	DRESSING
1 tablespoon sesame oil	125 ml (½ cup) olive oil
½ Chinese cabbage, sliced	125 ml (½ cup) balsamic vinegar
½ cup slivered almonds	60 g (2 oz) caster sugar
100 g (3½ oz) Chinese fried egg noodles, cooked	pinch of salt
4 shallots, finely chopped	2 tablespoons soy sauce
2 tomatoes, finely chopped	

Heat oil in a frying pan and fry chicken. Set aside to cool.

To make dressing, combine all ingredients in a bowl (or jar) and mix well (or put the lid on and shake).

To serve, place chicken, Chinese cabbage, almonds, egg noodles, shallots and tomatoes in a bowl. Toss to combine, pour over dressing and serve immediately.

prawn glass noodle salad

Serves 4

300 g medium cooked king prawns, peeled and deveined
125 g (4½ oz) dried bean thread noodles
75 g (2½ oz) carrots, peeled and cut into strips
75 g (2½ oz) Lebanese cucumber, shredded, seeds removed
1 small red onion, finely sliced
60 g (2 oz) snow pea sprouts
1 red capsicum, finely sliced
coriander leaves, to garnish

DRESSING
1 tablespoon natural pineapple juice
1 tablespoon lime zest, finely grated
3 tablespoons lime juice
1 tablespoon raw sugar
60 ml (2 fl oz) coconut milk
1 tablespoon fish sauce (nam pla)

Chop the prawns into halves or smaller pieces if you like.

Put the noodles into a large bowl and pour boiling water over to cover them. Let sit for 5-7 minutes then strain and run under cold water to stop cooking. Tip the noodles into a mixing bowl and allow to cool. Add all the other ingredients, except for the coriander leaves, and toss gently using hands.

Make the dressing by combining all the ingredients. Stir well to ensure the sugar is dissolved. Pour the dressing over the noodle ingredients and toss gently. Top with the coriander leaves and serve.

These noodles are sometimes called mung bean noodles. You can replace them with rice vermicelli noddles if you like.

fish and seafood

baked fish

Serves 4-6

1 large snapper, mullet or redfish, cleaned
1 teaspoon salt
¼ teaspoon white pepper
2 onions, sliced
4 ripe tomatoes, skinned and thickly sliced
½ teaspoon ground allspice (see glossary)
¼ teaspoon extra salt

¼ teaspoon black peppercorns, crushed
½ teaspoon cayenne pepper
2 tablespoons brown sugar
½ cup (4 fl oz) vinegar
¼ cup (2 fl oz) water
60 g (2 oz) butter

Preheat oven to 150°C (300°F). Place fish in a greased baking dish and season with salt and pepper. Cover with onion and tomato. Sprinkle with allspice, extra salt, peppercorns, cayenne pepper and brown sugar. Add vinegar and water and dot with small pieces of butter.

Bake fish in the oven for 20-30 minutes, depending on the size of fish. Baste frequently. Serve with a green salad or roasted vegetables.

crayfish mornay

Serves 2

1 x 1 kg (2 lb) crayfish	MORNAY SAUCE
1 shallot (green onion), finely chopped	15 g (½ oz) butter
salt and freshly ground black pepper, to taste	1 tablespoon plain (all-purpose) flour
cayenne pepper, to taste	⅔ cup (5½ fl oz) milk
paprika, to taste	60 g (2 oz) gruyère cheese, grated
30 g (1 oz) butter	salt and freshly ground black pepper, to taste
parsley sprigs, to garnish	1-2 tablespoons fresh cream

Wash crayfish well under warm water, then remove its head and cut the shell in half, removing the intestines at the same time. Scoop meat from shell and cut into 2 cm (1 in) cubes. Place shell halves in a hot oven 220°C (425°F) until they are bright red in colour.

Place crayfish meat into a bowl, and add shallot, salt and pepper, and a dash of cayenne pepper. Mix gently. Place mixture in hot shells, sprinkle with paprika, dot with butter and place under a hot grill until the meat becomes opaque white and loses its transparent appearance. Coat with mornay sauce, and replace under hot grill briefly, until golden brown – overcooking will toughen the crayfish.

To make mornay sauce, melt butter in a small saucepan. Blend in flour until smooth, then cook for 1-2 minutes. Add milk and bring to the boil, stirring continuously. Remove pan from heat and add cheese. Stir until cheese melts. Season with salt and pepper and add enough cream to make the sauce a good coating consistency.

Serve garnished with parsley sprigs. Goes well with thinly sliced fried potatoes and sautéed mushrooms.

deep-fried fish

Serves 4

4 fillets of fish
(shark, whiting, garfish, flathead,
snapper, mulloway, trevally, cod or trout)

lemon wedges to garnish
tartare sauce

BATTER
1 cup plain (all-purpose) flour
pinch of salt
60 g (2 oz) melted butter
2 eggs, lightly beaten
1 cup (8 fl oz) beer
1 egg white, stiffly beaten
extra plain (all-purpose) flour, for coating fish
olive oil, for frying

To make the batter, combine flour, salt, butter and eggs. Gradually add beer and stir until smooth. Cover and stand for one hour in a warm place. Just before using, fold in egg white (this makes a light, fluffy batter). Flour fish and coat with batter.

To deep-fry fish, heat enough oil to cover fish in a deep frying pan or electric fryer. Test temperature by putting a 2.5 cm (1 in) cube of bread in the pan – it should brown in one minute when the oil is at the correct temperature. Place coated fish in oil, avoiding contact between pieces. Cook fish for about five minutes. Drain well on absorbent paper.

Serve piping hot with lemon wedges and tartare sauce.

fried lobster

Serves 2

1 medium-sized rock lobster	olive oil, for frying
½ teaspoon salt	juice from half a lemon
1 teaspoon plain (all-purpose) flour	lemon wedges and finely chopped parsley, to garnish

Cut lobster in half lengthways and remove the bag in the head and the intestine.

Sprinkle lobster meat with salt and flour. Heat olive oil in a pan and add lobster, cut side down. Fry for 15 minutes, then turn and fry for another 15 minutes. Drain and place lobster on plate and squeeze over lemon juice.

Garnish with lemon wedges and serve with tossed salad greens.

fried whitebait

Serves 4

500 g (1 lb) fresh whitebait	rock salt, crushed
plain (all purpose) flour, for coating	sliced lemon and fresh bread and
olive oil for frying	butter, for serving

Rinse whitebait and drain well, then dry with absorbent paper. Toss lightly in flour and place in a wire basket. Fry in deep, hot oil. Drain well.

Reheat oil and fry whitebait again, until very crisp. Drain on absorbent paper again, then sprinkle with rock salt and serve with lemon and bread and butter.

lobster thermidor

Serves 4

90 g (3 oz) butter
30 g (1 oz) plain (all-purpose) flour
1 cup (8 fl oz) milk
2 tablespoons thickened cream
½ teaspoon Dijon mustard
salt and black pepper, to taste

2 medium-sized cooked lobsters,
meat removed from shells and diced
1 shallot (green onion), finely chopped
2 tablespoons white wine or sherry
60 g (2 oz) Parmesan cheese, grated

In a saucepan, melt 30 g (1 oz) butter. Add flour, mix well and cook gently for about two minutes. Stir in milk, cream, mustard and salt and pepper. Add lobster meat and heat gently.

In another pan, melt remaining butter and fry onion or shallot. Add to lobster mixture, together with wine. Pile mixture into lobster shells, cover tops with grated Parmesan cheese and brown under a hot grill.

fish fillets in cheese sauce

Serves 4

750 g (1½ lb) fish fillets
(John Dory, flathead or blackfish)
salt and black pepper, to taste
1 x 420 g (13½ oz) can cream of celery
or mushroom soup

125 g (4 oz) cheddar cheese, grated
¼ cup (2 fl oz) sherry
¼ teaspoon paprika

Preheat oven to 180°C (350°F).

Cut fish into serving pieces, removing skin and bones. Season with salt and pepper. Place in a buttered ovenproof casserole dish. In a bowl, combine celery or mushroom soup, cheese and sherry. Pour over fish. Sprinkle with paprika and bake for 25 minutes.

oysters mornay

Serves 1-2

12 large, flat oysters
salt and pepper, to taste
1 tablespoon Parmesan cheese, grated

MORNAY SAUCE
15 g (½ oz) butter
1 tablespoon plain (all-purpose) flour
⅔ cup (5½ fl oz) milk
60 g (2 oz) gruyère cheese, grated
salt and freshly ground black pepper, to taste
1-2 tablespoons fresh cream

Preheat oven to 180°C (350°F).

Sprinkle oysters with salt and pepper and place under a hot grill for one minute. Spread each oyster with mornay sauce to cover. Sprinkle with Parmesan cheese and bake in a hot oven for about 10 minutes or until golden brown. Serve immediately.

To make mornay sauce, melt butter in a small saucepan. Blend in flour until smooth, then cook for about two minutes. Add milk and bring to the boil, stirring continuously. Remove pan from heat and add cheese. Stir until cheese melts. Season with salt and pepper and add enough cream to make the sauce a good coating consistency.

poached fish in white wine sauce

Serves 4

750 g–1 kg (1½–2 lb) fish fillets
(bream or sole), skinned and boned
1½ cups (12 fl oz) dry white wine
pinch of tarragon
1 small onion, finely chopped
3 egg yolks
3 tablespoons fresh cream
salt and pepper, to taste

COURT BOUILLON
1½ cups (12 fl oz) water
½ cup (4 fl oz) white wine
juice of 1 lemon
1 onion, chopped
½ stick of celery, chopped
1 clove garlic, finely chopped
1 teaspoon black peppercorns
4–5 sprigs thyme
1 bay leaf

To make the court bouillon, combine all ingredients in a saucepan and bring to the boil over high heat. Reduce heat and simmer for eight minutes. Cool mixture slightly, remove peppercorn, thyme and bay leaf, then purée in a blender or food processor, then return to the saucepan and gently bring to the boil.

Poach fish in court bouillon for 12–20 minutes. The fish should be opaque when cooked. Drain well and keep hot. Place wine, tarragon and onion in a saucepan and bring to the boil. Add court bouillon and boil continuously, until volume is reduced by half. Allow to cool.

In a bowl, beat egg yolks with cream. Add to cooled liquid and reheat gently, without boiling. Season with salt and pepper, pour over the poached fish fillets, and serve.

seafood chowder

Serves 4-6

MARINARA MIX
500 g (1 lb) marinara mix
(fish pieces, shelled prawns/shrimp,
oysters, scallops, crab), washed

30 g (1 oz) butter
½ teaspoon saffron (optional – see glossary)
salt, to taste
1 cup (8 fl oz) milk
1 onion, sliced
3 cups (24 fl oz) water
1 potato, sliced
¼–½ cup (2-4 fl oz) fresh cream
salt and freshly ground black pepper, to taste
1 tablespoon parsley, finely chopped, to garnish

Poach marinara mix in salted water until just tender. Strain cooking liquid, taking care to remove any skin or bones from fish, and set aside. Reserve seafood for later.

Melt butter in a saucepan and sauté onion and potato for two minutes. Add strained cooking liquid, saffron and salt. Simmer for 20 minutes, then purée in a blender or food processor until smooth.

Return soup to saucepan, add milk and bring to the boil. Add cream and seafood and season to taste. Heat gently but do not boil.

Sprinkle with parsley and serve with crusty French bread.

seafood paella

Serves 8

¼ cup (2 fl oz) olive oil
2 tablespoons butter
2 cloves garlic, chopped
1 onion, chopped
1 red capsicum (bell pepper), seeded and chopped
3 tomatoes, peeled
330 g (10½ oz) short grain rice
3¼ cups (26 fl oz) fish stock
1 teaspoon salt

½ teaspoon saffron threads, crumbled (see glossary)
500 g (1 lb) mixture of seafood (prawns/shrimp, scallops, mussels, uncooked crab), washed, peeled, debearded and deveined
¼ teaspoon freshly ground black pepper
3 tablespoons fresh parsley, chopped
2 teaspoons fresh oregano, chopped
1 teaspoon fresh thyme, chopped

In a large, deep frying pan (that has a lid), heat oil and butter over a medium heat. Add garlic, onion and capsicum, and cook until tender (about 10 minutes). Stir in tomatoes and cook for about five minutes. Add rice and stir, then stir in fish stock, salt and saffron. Cover and bring to boil, then remove lid, reduce heat and simmer for five minutes, stirring continually. Add seafood, then cover and simmer for a further five minutes. Add pepper, parsley, oregano, thyme and cook, still covered, until tender. Serve hot with crusty French bread.

tuna mornay

Serves 4

500 g (1 lb) potatoes, boiled
30 g (1 oz) margarine
2 tablespoons milk
salt and pepper, to taste
425 g (13½ oz) can tuna in brine
30-60 g (2-3 oz) tasty cheese, grated

BÉCHAMEL SAUCE
1¼ cups (10 fl oz) milk
1 onion, quartered
1 stalk celery, chopped
1 carrot, chopped
6 black peppercorns
1 blade of mace (see glossary)
1 bay leaf
2 cloves
30 g (1 oz) butter
2 tablespoons plain (all-purpose) flour
salt and freshly ground black pepper, to taste

Preheat oven to 180°C (350°F).

Mash potatoes and beat in margarine, milk and salt and pepper. Line sides and bottom of a shallow ovenproof dish with mashed potato, then top with flaked tuna.

To make béchamel sauce, place milk, onion, celery, carrot, peppercorns, mace, bay leaf and cloves in the top of a double boiler over gently boiling water. Cover the pan and heat very slowly for 30 minutes. Strain and set milk aside. Melt butter in a heavy saucepan, stir in flour and cook for one minute over a medium heat. Add milk and heat, stirring constantly until boiling. Reduce heat to low and cook for two minutes. Season with salt and pepper.

Stir cheese into béchamel sauce, spoon sauce over tuna, and bake in a moderate oven for 15 minutes or until golden on top.

salt and pepper squid

Serves 1

1 whole squid
1 tablespoon salt and pepper
vegetable oil, for deep-frying
1 cup cornflour
4–5 cloves garlic, finely sliced

1 long chilli, chopped (remove seeds if you want to minimise the spiciness)
2 shallots (spring onions/scallions), green section only, chopped

Clean the squid, cut the tubes open and cut a cross-hatch pattern into the insides. Be careful not to cut all the way through.

Cut the tubes into 4 x 2 cm (2 x 1 in) pieces and place in a mixing bowl with one pinch of the salt and pepper mixture, mix well.

Heat the oil in a deep fryer to 180°C (350°F).

Put the cornflour in a bowl and slowly add in enough water to make a batter with a consistency that is thicker than paint and slightly sticky. Then add in the squid. Use your whole hand to mix the squid with the batter, don't just coat the surface.

Slowly lower the squid into the hot oil, it should float when ready. Remove from the oil immediately. Lightly oil a wok, place over high heat, throw in the garlic for a good stir and then the chilli and shallots. Finally add the squid, sprinkle with some of the salt and pepper mixture and give it all a good toss. Serve with some of the remaining mixture on the side.

Use as little oil as possible when tossing the shallots, garlic and chilli. You don't want any excess oil to be absorbed into the batter. A good trick is to use a spray vegetable oil, or rub a paper towel with a little oil on it over the wok.

wok fried prawns in basil and chilli

Serves 2

½ kg (1 lb) tiger prawns, uncooked, in their shells | 1 bunch basil leaves
1 cup (8 fl oz) Balsamic vinegar | 1 whole red chilli
5 tablespoons olive oil | 1 small red chilli deseeded chopped (to taste)
3 cloves garlic crushed | juice of one lemon

Marinate overnight or for at least an hour the tiger prawns in their shells with the vinegar and 3 tablespoons olive oil and garlic. Tear the basil leaves and mix with the whole chilli and chopped chilli.

Heat the wok with 2 tablespoons of olive oil until smoking. Add the chilli and stir. Add the tiger prawns and the marinade to the wok and stir once. Add the basil last. Stir until the prawns are pink.

Serve into a large plate and pour over the lemon juice. Serve finger bowls of water and lemon juice with the prawns and fresh crust bread. (You can peel the prawns before serving and pour the juices over them on the plate if you prefer.)

thai fish and squash curry

Serves 4

1 tablespoon of olive oil	500 g (1 lb) firm fish fillets, cut into pieces
1 large red onion, sliced into thin wedges	500 g (1 lb) golden squash
½ red capsicum, thinly sliced	100 g (3½ oz) sheep's yoghurt
1 garlic clove, crushed	2 cups water or fish stock
2 teaspoons red curry paste	1 cup shredded basil leaves
½ teaspoon brown sugar	1 cup coriander (cilantro) leaves
1 tablespoon fish sauce	juice of 1 lime
	2 teaspoons lime zest

Heat oil in wok or large frying pan. Add onion, capsicum and garlic and cook for 1-2 minutes.

Stir in red curry paste and sugar and cook for 1 minute, until fragrant.

Add fish sauce and cook through for a minute.

Add fish, squash, yoghurt and water or fish stock and cook for about 5-10 minutes or until cooked, stirring occasionally. Remove from heat, add the herbs, lime juice and zest and stir through gently.

Serve with steamed vegetables.

fishcakes

250 g (8 oz) white fish, poached or steamed
250 g (8 oz) mashed potatoes
1 egg
Salt and freshly ground black pepper, to taste
30-60 g (1-2 oz) butter for frying
Parsley and lemon, to garnish

COATING
15-30 g (½-1 oz) seasoned flour (see glossary)
1 egg, beaten
3-4 tablespoons crisp breadcrumbs

Remove all bones and skin from the fish, then flake with a fork. In a bowl, place fish, potato, egg and seasoning.

Mix well, then divide into 8 round cakes.

Coat the fishcakes in seasoned flour, then egg, then breadcrumbs.

Heat butter in a frying pan and fry fishcakes for 2-3 minutes, until golden brown on the underside. Turn, then cook for the same time on the second side. Lift out of pan and drain on absorbent paper.

Serve hot, garnished with parsley and lemon.

thai fishcakes with sweet chilli sauce and cucumber relish

Serves 4-6

	SPICY CUCUMBER RELISH
500 g (1 lb) white fish fillets, finely diced	*Makes 2 cups*
2 tablespoons red curry paste	1 cup (8 fl oz) coconut or white vinegar
2 tablespoons fish sauce	1 cup white sugar
1 tablespoon cornflour	splash of fish sauce
1 egg, beaten	1 large continental cucumber
½ cup finely sliced green beans	4 small red chillies, finely chopped
¼ cup finely sliced spring onion	½ cup roasted, unsalted peanuts, crushed or
vegetable oil for deep-frying	finely chopped
½ cup sweet chilli sauce	⅓ cup chopped coriander, including stems
½ cup spicy cucumber relish	

In a food processor, mince fish to a paste. Add curry paste, fish sauce, cornflour and egg. Combine well. Transfer to a bowl and mix in beans and onions. Wet hands and shape mix into flat round cakes approximately 5 cm (2 in) in diameter and 1 cm (½ in) thick. Deep-fry in vegetable oil until golden brown, about 5-7 minutes. Drain on paper towel. Serve with sweet chilli sauce and cucumber relish.

The secret to fishcakes is not to overwork the fish mixture, otherwise the cakes will be tough and chewy.

CUCUMBER RELISH

Combine the vinegar, sugar and fish sauce in a small saucepan over medium heat. Bring to a gentle boil, stirring occasionally, and cook for 1 minute. Remove from heat and cool to room temperature. Peel cucumber, scrape out seeds and cut into small dice. Place the cucumber, chillies, peanuts and coriander in a bowl.

Pour over dressing and toss gently. (The dressing can be made one day in advance and refrigerated. Then added to relish ingredients just before serving.)

seafood laksa

Serves 4

3 cups coconut milk
2 tablespoons Laksa Paste
3 cups chicken stock
1 teaspoon palm sugar
2 tablespoons fish sauce
allow 150 g (5 oz) mixed seafood per person
250 g (8 oz) fresh Chinese egg noodles or rice noodles if preferred

½ cup chopped laksa leaf (Vietnamese mint)
100 g (3½ oz) bean sprouts
2 tablespoons crispy-fried shallots
2 spring onions, finely diced
4 lime wedges

Skim the thick cream off the top of the coconut milk. Heat the cream to a simmer in a large saucepan. Add Laksa Paste and fry until fragrant, about 5 minutes. Add remaining coconut milk and stock. Bring to the boil. Add palm sugar and fish sauce.

Add seafood, reduce heat and poach gently until cooked, about 3-4 minutes. Blanch noodles in boiling water and divide between four serving bowls. Pour on laksa and garnish with remaining ingredients.

The famous Malaysian national dish is a deliciously satisfying meal in itself.

meat dishes

beef stroganoff

Serves 4

90 g (3 oz) butter	1½ teaspoons salt
1 large onion, thinly sliced	freshly ground black pepper, to taste
250 g (8 oz) mushrooms, peeled and sliced	pinch of nutmeg
750 g (1½ lb) fillet steak,	300 g (10 oz) sour cream
trimmed of fat and cut into thin strips	parsley, chopped, to garnish

Melt half the butter in a heavy frying pan and sauté onion until soft. Add mushrooms and cook for five minutes. Place mixture in a bowl and keep warm.

Melt remaining butter in pan and quickly brown beef strips on all sides. Do this stage in two lots unless you have a very large frying pan. Take pan off the heat and add onion, mushrooms, salt, pepper and nutmeg. Stir well to blend, then replace pan over a medium heat and pour in sour cream. Stir gently until heated through. Do not allow sauce to boil.

Serve with boiled rice, cooked cabbage or coleslaw.

chicken teriyaki kebabs

Serves 4

2 tablespoons butter
⅓ cup (2¾ fl oz) teriyaki sauce or soy sauce
2.5 cm (1 in) piece ginger, chopped
2 tablespoons sugar
bamboo skewers, soaked in water for 10 minutes

2 tablespoons dry sherry
500 g (1 lb) boneless chicken breasts, skinned
4 small onions, roughly chopped into chunks
1 shallot (green onion), chopped

Place butter, teriyaki sauce, ginger, sugar and dry sherry in a small pan and stir over a medium heat until sugar is dissolved. Allow to cool.

Cut chicken into 2.5 cm (1 in) pieces and stir into marinade with shallots. Chill for at least two hours.

Thread chicken and onion onto bamboo skewers and grill for about five minutes on either side, or until cooked, brushing occasionally with marinade.

Serve with steamed rice and salad.

chilli con carne

Serves 4

2 tablespoon olive oil	pinch of cayenne pepper
1 large onion, chopped	2 teaspoons paprika
1 green capsicum (bell pepper), seeds and pith removed and chopped	500 g (1 lb) minced (ground) or diced beef
1 stick celery, chopped	250 g (8 oz) tomatoes
1 tablespoon chilli powder (optional)	250 g (8 oz) cooked kidney beans or soaked and cooked haricot beans
½ teaspoon salt	⅔ cup (5½ fl oz) water

Heat oil in a saucepan. Add onion, capsicum and celery and fry until just tender, then add other ingredients. Bring just to the boil, then lower the heat and cook gently for about 55 minutes (for minced meat) or 1¼ hours (for diced meat). Stir halfway through cooking, and add a little more water if necessary.

Goes well with rice or corn chips.

Note: You can also add 60 g (2 oz) cooked rice to the recipe.

curried chicken

Serves 6

60 g (2 oz) butter
1 x 1.5 kg (3 lb) whole chicken, cut into pieces
2 onions, chopped
1 tablespoon curry powder
1 teaspoon curry paste
1 tablespoon plain (all-purpose) flour

2 cups (16 fl oz) chicken stock
1 clove garlic, crushed
salt and freshly ground black pepper, to taste
1 tablespoon redcurrant jelly
½ cup (4 fl oz) coconut milk
¼ cup (2 fl oz) fresh cream

Preheat oven to 180°C (350°F). Melt butter in a flameproof casserole dish (use one that has a lid) and fry chicken until golden brown. Remove chicken and sauté onion in remaining butter until golden. Add curry powder and paste and continue to cook for about four minutes. Add flour and blend until smooth. Stirring continuously, add stock and bring to the boil. Replace chicken in casserole, add garlic and season with salt and pepper.

Cover casserole dish and cook in the oven for 45 minutes, or until chicken is tender. Place chicken on a serving dish and keep warm. Add redcurrant jelly and coconut milk to curry sauce, bring to the boil and simmer for five minutes. Take off the heat, stir in cream and spoon sauce over chicken pieces.

Serve with boiled rice and chutney.

fillet mignon

Serves 4

4 bacon rashers, rind removed
4 slices of fillet steak, 3.5 cm (2½ in) thick
salt and freshly ground black pepper, to taste

PARSLEY BUTTER
60 g (2 oz) butter, room temperature
1 teaspoon parsley, finely chopped
2 teaspoons lemon juice

Wrap a bacon rasher around each fillet and secure with a toothpick. Preheat grill to hot and brush rack with oil. Place fillet under grill rack 8 cm (3¼ in) below heat. Grill for about four minutes on each side for rare steak, about five minutes each side for medium-rare steak. Turn fillets gently so you don't pierce the meat and let the juices escape. Season with salt and pepper and serve immediately.

To make the parsley butter, beat butter in a bowl until light and creamy. Beat in parsley and lemon juice. Chill well before serving.

Garnish with parsley butter and serve immediately.

lamb shanks

Serves 6

6 lamb shanks	1 cup (8 fl oz) red wine
4 tablespoons olive oil	2 tablespoons Worcestershire sauce
2 medium onions, diced	2 tablespoons sesame seeds
2 carrots, julienned	2 tablespoons honey
4 cloves garlic	75 g (2½ oz) macadamia nuts, crushed
2 tablespoons sugar	salt and freshly ground black pepper, to taste
1 cup (8 fl oz) white vinegar	bunch of fresh coriander (cilantro),
1 x 400 g (13 oz) can tomatoes, diced	finely chopped

Preheat oven to 150-180°C (300–350°F). Brown lamb shanks in a frying pan with two tablespoons of oil, then place in an ovenproof casserole dish.

Heat remaining oil in frying pan. Add onions, carrots and garlic and sauté. When they start to brown, add sugar and vinegar. Lower heat and simmer uncovered for 15 minutes, so that mixture reduces.

Add tomatoes to mixture. Bring to the boil and add red wine, Worcestershire sauce and sesame seeds. Stir in honey, macadamia nuts and salt and pepper. Transfer mixture to the casserole dish, making sure it covers the lamb shanks. Sprinkle with coriander.

Cover the casserole dish with foil and cook in the oven for at least two hours. The longer it cooks, the more tender the lamb will be.

roast beef

Serves 6

1 x 1.5 kg (3 lb) rolled sirloin of beef
salt and freshly ground black pepper, to taste

butter or olive oil, for frying
1¼ cups (10 fl oz) beef stock

Preheat oven to 165°C (330°F). Rub meat with salt and pepper and place in a roasting pan, fat side up. If the meat has little fat, add one or two tablespoons of butter or oil to the pan. Place beef in the oven and cook for two hours.

Remove roast beef to a hot carving platter and leave to stand in a warm place for 10 minutes before carving.

To make gravy, add beef stock to pan juices and bring to the boil. Strain into gravy boat and serve with beef and roast vegetables.

roast chicken

Serves 6

1.5 kg (3 lb) whole chicken, washed and dried
salt and freshly ground black pepper, to taste

3 tablespoons olive oil
1¼ cups (10 fl oz) chicken stock

Preheat oven to 180°C (350°F). Rub chicken with salt, pepper and half the olive oil. Truss (see glossary) chicken and place in a greased roasting pan with remaining oil. Cook in the oven, basting occasionally, for one hour, or until tender and golden brown all over. Remove chicken and keep warm.

To make the gravy, add chicken stock to pan juices and bring to the boil. Strain into a gravy boat. Goes well with roast potatoes and green vegetables.

saltimbocca

Serves 4

8 thin veal steaks	2 tablespoons dry white wine or marsala
125 g (4 oz) ham, thinly sliced	(see glossary)
½ teaspoon dried sage or 8 fresh sage leaves	2 tablespoons beef stock
30 g (1 oz) butter	½ teaspoon salt
	freshly ground black pepper, to taste

Place veal slices between two sheets of plastic clingwrap and flatten with a rolling pin or the side of a meat mallet. Place a slice of ham, cut the same size as the veal, on each fillet of steak. Place a sage leaf or a light sprinkling of dried sage on top of the ham. Roll up veal and ham and fasten rolls with toothpicks.

Melt butter in a frying pan that has a lid and brown rolls on all sides (about 10 minutes). Reduce heat and add wine and stock. Add salt and pepper, stir to lift pan juices, cover tightly and simmer very gently for 20 minutes, turning rolls occasionally, until veal is tender and liquid is reduced to a glaze. Serve immediately.

Serve with risotto and a tossed salad.

southern fried chicken

Serves 4-6

1.5 kg (3 lb) whole chicken, cut into pieces
60 g (2 oz) plain (all-purpose) flour
salt and freshly ground black pepper, to taste

1 teaspoon paprika (optional)
125 g (4 oz) butter or olive oil, for frying

Soak chicken in salted water for 10 minutes. Shake off excess water.

In a large paper bag, shake flour, salt and pepper and paprika (if using) together to mix. Put chicken pieces in the bag and shake thoroughly to coat.

In a large frying pan, heat butter and fry all chicken pieces together over a high heat until golden brown on one side. Turn pieces over, lower heat and continue to fry, turning occasionally, until meat is tender (30-40 minutes, depending on size of pieces).

Serve hot with coleslaw or potato salad.

steak diane

Serves 4

4 slices of fillet steak cut 2.5 cm (1 in) thick	1 tablespoon tomato sauce
30 g (1 oz) butter	1 teaspoon Worcestershire sauce
2 cloves garlic, crushed	¼ cup (2 fl oz) water
salt and freshly ground black pepper, to taste	1 teaspoon cornflour (cornstarch), mixed with a little cold water

Slit steaks horizontally through to the centre and open out meat to create a butterfly fillet. Flatten steaks with the side of a meat mallet to 5 mm (¼ in) thickness.

Melt half the butter in a heavy frying pan, add one crushed garlic clove and fry two of the steaks quickly — about 40 seconds on each side for rare steak and one minute each side for medium steak. Add remaining butter and garlic to the pan when cooking the other steaks (most frying pans will probably hold only two steaks at a time). Season cooked steaks with salt and pepper and keep aside on a warm platter.

Add sauces and water to frying pan and stir into pan juices over a medium heat. Thicken with cornflour paste and bring to the boil. Pour sauce over steaks.

Serve with new potatoes and a tossed green salad.

veal cordon bleu

Serves 4

8 medium-sized veal steaks	1 egg, beaten with 1 tablespoon water
4 thin slices ham (about size of steaks)	breadcrumbs, for coating
4 thin slices gruyère cheese	oil, for frying
seasoned flour (see glossary), for coating	lemon wedges, to garnish

Flatten veal steaks between two sheets of plastic clingwrap by beating with the side of a meat mallet or a rolling pin. Put the steaks in pairs, so that pieces in a pair are of a similar size. Place a slice of ham and a slice of cheese between each pair of steaks, keeping ham and cheese 5 mm (¼ in) in from edge of the veal all round. Gently beat edges to seal. Coat veal with seasoned flour, dip carefully in egg, then coat with breadcrumbs, pressing them on firmly.

Allow to stand for 10 minutes, then heat oil in a frying pan and shallow fry veal over a moderate heat until light golden brown. Turn carefully and brown other side. It will take about five minutes to completely cook the veal. Drain on absorbent paper and serve piping hot.

Garnish with lemon wedges and serve with boiled new potatoes and vegetables.

Note: If cheese leaks out of the steak and causes spitting,
place a slice of raw potato in the pan — it will absorb moisture.

veal with mozzarella

Serves 4

750 g (1½ lb) veal steak, thinly sliced
seasoned flour (see glossary)
1 egg, beaten with ¼ cup (2 fl oz) water
125 g (4 oz) fine breadcrumbs mixed with
30 g (1 oz) Parmesan cheese, grated
olive oil, for frying
2 tablespoons extra olive oil
2 cloves garlic, crushed

1 onion, finely chopped
1 x 400 g (13 oz) can tomatoes, peeled
3 tablespoons tomato paste
¼ teaspoon dried thyme
½ teaspoon caster (superfine) sugar
salt and freshly ground black pepper, to taste
250 g (8 oz) mozzarella cheese, thinly sliced

Preheat oven to 180°C (350°F).

Flatten veal slices lightly, using the side of a meat mallet. Dip in seasoned flour, then in combined egg and water, and then coat with combined breadcrumbs and Parmesan cheese. Press crumbs on firmly.

Heat oil in a frying pan and fry veal until golden brown on both sides. Drain on absorbent paper.

Heat extra oil in a saucepan, then add garlic and onion and sauté for five minutes. Add tomatoes, tomato paste, thyme, sugar and salt and pepper. Cover, and simmer for 10 minutes.

Pour one-third of tomato mixture into an ovenproof casserole dish. Arrange veal on top, cover with cheese and pour over remaining sauce. Cook, uncovered, in the oven for 30 35 minutes.

Serve with a tossed green salad.

veal scallopine marsala

Serves 4

4 very thin veal steaks, cut in half	45 g (1½ oz) butter
salt and freshly ground black pepper, to taste	½ cup (4 fl oz) dry marsala (see glossary)
2 eggs, beaten	or sherry
3 tablespoons plain (all-purpose) flour	½ cup (4 fl oz) beef stock

Sprinkle veal steaks with salt and pepper. Dip steaks in egg, then coat lightly with flour and set aside.

Melt half the butter in a frying pan and cover base completely. Add steaks (most frying pans will fit two steaks) and brown meat, taking care not to burn it, for about five minutes on each side. When well browned, add half the marsala and swirl steaks in liquid so it will thicken itself with the flour and butter. Remove steaks to warm plates. Repeat with remaining steaks.

Add stock and remaining butter to pan. Scrape base and sides to include all leftover bits in sauce. Pour sauce over meat and serve.

vienna schnitzel

Serves 4

4 thinly cut veal steaks
1 clove garlic, crushed
1 tablespoon lemon juice
salt and freshly ground black pepper, to taste
plain (all-purpose) flour, for coating

1 egg, beaten with 1 tablespoon water
breadcrumbs, for coating
olive oil, for frying
1 hard-boiled egg, anchovy fillets, capers,
lemon slices and fresh parsley, to garnish

Flatten veal between two pieces of plastic clingwrap, using the side of a meat mallet or rolling pin. Cut skin on edges to prevent curling during cooking. Lay veal on a plate and set aside.

Mix garlic with lemon juice and brush onto veal. Season with salt and pepper and allow to stand for 30 minutes. Dip each veal steak into flour, then egg, and finally breadcrumbs, pressing them firmly on to coat veal completely. Refrigerate for 1 hour.

Heat oil in a frying pan and shallow fry veal steaks over a moderate heat for about two minutes on either side, or until golden brown. Lift veal onto absorbent paper to drain, then place on a hot serving platter.

Garnish each schnitzel with a slice of hard-boiled egg and top with a rolled anchovy fillet, a few capers, a slice of lemon and fresh parsley.

Serve with boiled new potatoes, sauerkraut and a tossed salad.

~~Pork Ribs~~ SOLD OUT $6⁰⁰

Shanks $5⁰⁰

Bratwurst $7⁰⁰

Hot / Sweet Italian Sausage

Hot / Mild Breakfast Sausage $

Ground Pork

Beef + Cheese Sausage $

100% GRASS-FED BEEF
_____

Ground Beef (Bulk) $6⁰⁰

Ground Beef Patties $6⁰⁰

chicken with corn and mango salsa

Serves 4

FOR THE CHICKEN
400 g (13 oz) cooked skinless, boneless chicken breast
1 bag mixed baby lettuce leaves
20 cooked asparagus tips
1 cup cooked unpeeled potatoes, diced

FOR THE SALSA
1 cup mango flesh, diced
1 cup corn kernels, canned or bottled
1 very small red onion, finely diced
1 small banana chilli, deseeded and minced
1 tablespoon coriander
chopped salt and ground black pepper to taste
3 tablespoons apple cider vinegar
1 tablespoon mustard seed oil

Cut the chicken meat into bite-sized pieces and set to one side.

Divide the lettuce leaves onto four plates. Top with equal amounts of asparagus, potatoes and chicken.

Make the salsa by combining all ingredients and stirring well. Spoon the salsa over the salad ingredients and serve immediately.

chicken burger

Serves 4

1kg (2lb) chicken mince (ground chicken)
1 egg, lightly beaten
40g (1½ oz) breadcrumbs
2 teaspoon grated fresh ginger

1 clove garlic, crushed
4 spring onions (scallions), finely chopped
handful coriander (cilantro) leaves, chopped
sea salt and pepper
bread of your choice

Place all of the ingredients in a large bowl and mix well until combined. Your hands are the best tool for the job. Form the mixture into patties about the size of your palm. Heat a little oil in a fry pan and cook the patties on medium-high heat for a few minutes on each side or until cooked through. Alternatively, you could cook them on the barbeque.

Serve on any type of bread (you may like to toast/grill it first) with any of the suggested accompaniments.

Suggested accompaniments: sweet chilli sauce or satay sauce, sliced cucumber, sliced tomato, grated carrot, fresh coriander (cilantro) leaves.

lamb koftas with minted yoghurt in pita bread

Serves 6

800 g (2 lb) minced lamb (ground lamb)
1 egg, lightly beaten
1 small onion, finely chopped
1 clove garlic, crushed
1 teaspoon ground cumin
1 teaspoon ground coriander
¼ teaspoon cinnamon
small handful of mint or coriander (cilantro), chopped
sea salt and pepper

TO SERVE
1 cup plain yoghurt
small handful mint leaves, chopped
1 tub of store-bought hummus
1 tub of store-bought tabouleh
pita bread

Combine all ingredients in a large bowl and mix well until all ingredients are incorporated. Your hands are the ideal tools for the job.

Form the mixture into 12 long sausages. You could insert wooden skewers at this point but the koftas will be bulkier to store.

Insert a skewer down the centre of each kofta then cook them on the barbecue (or cook under the grill or in a frypan if you prefer).

Combine the yoghurt and mint in a small bowl. Place the hummus and tabouleh in two more bowls, place the pita bread on a plate and stack the cooked koftas on another plate. Everyone can help themselves to make their own lunch, filling up their pita breads with the various components.

This is a great meal to feed a large crowd. It looks impressive and tastes delicious. You could also serve them on a bed of flavoured couscous and top with a dollop each of minted yoghurt and hummus.

mediterranean lamb burgers

Makes 4 burgers

YOGHURT SAUCE
200 g (7 oz) plain low fat yoghurt
1 garlic clove, crushed
¼ teaspoon sea salt
3 teaspoon fresh mint leaves, shredded

BURGERS
1 kg (2 lb) lamb mince (ground lamb),
from the shoulder
1 garlic clove, crushed
1 tablespoon chopped fresh rosemary
1 tablespoon chopped fresh parsley
salt and pepper to taste

SALAD
⅓ cup kalamata olives, seeded and coarsely chopped
2 ripe medium tomatoes, coarsely chopped
3 tablespoons chopped fresh parsley
2 tablespoons olive oil
2 tablespoons apple cider vinegar
¼ cup low fat feta or goat cheese, crumbled (optional)
4 wholemeal pita bread, split in half

Combine the yoghurt ingredients into a bowl and mix thoroughly. Set aside.

Preheat the barbecue or a frying pan and brush with a little olive oil. Combine all the lamb ingredients in a bowl and cook in the frying pan for 6 minutes each side, or until medium to rare.

To make the salad, combine olives, tomatoes, parsley, olive oil and apple cider vinegar in a bowl. Season with salt and pepper.

Transfer burgers to pita pockets and sprinkle with feta or goat cheese. Serve with yoghurt sauce and salad.

For a no-carbohydrates option, serve the burger with yoghurt sauce and the salad on the side, without the bread.

sweet chicken curry

(Mild to medium)

2 medium onions, diced	½ cup coconut
1 tablespoon garlic, minced	½ bag tropical mix
1 apple, peeled and diced	spices from your kitchen
½ jar curry paste	1.25 kg (2.7 lb) chicken
1 can coconut cream	handful coriander
1 tablespoon plum jam	your choice of fresh vegetables

Heat onion and garlic in oil until translucent. Add apple and curry paste cook and cook a few minutes. Add coconut cream, plum jam, coconut, tropical mix and curry spices and bring to the boil.

Remove the bones from the chicken and dice into bite sizes bits. Add the chicken and bring to the boil again while cutting up the coriander finely, only use the leaf unless you like a strong coriander taste. Turn the heat down and simmer for 45 minutes, then cool in the pot then transfer into a suitable container. Place in the fridge. The curry should not be eaten for 24 hours.

Serve with a fresh green vegetables (snow peas, boc choy etc) and rice. Add saffron to the rice for yellow, or for flavour you can cook the rice with dill or the coriander roots.

Coarse bread goes very well with this wet curry which should be medium hot. If you desire a warmer curry, try adding a hot curry sauce or add more curry powder, Tabasco or fresh chili, but this should also be added the day before and left for the 24 hours.

beef or lamb curry

(Medium to hot)

2 medium onions, diced	½ cup coconut
1 parsnip, chopped	½ bag tropical mix
1 tablespoon garlic	1 banana
cooking oil	2 tablespoons peanut butter
1 apple, peeled and diced	2 tablespoons red currant jam
2 tablespoons raisins	1 tablespoon lemon juice
½ jar curry paste	1 kg (2 lb) diced beef or lamb
1 or more teaspoons chili powder	curry powder and spices to taste
1 can coconut cream	1 cup water (if required)
1 can hot curry sauce	

Heat onions, parsnip and garlic in oil. Add apple, raisins, curry paste and chili powder then cook a few minutes.

Stir in the coconut cream, curry sauce, red currant jam, coconut, tropical mix, banana, peanut butter and lemon juice, bring to the boil.

Add the beef/lamb and simmer for 45 minutes, then cool in the pot and transfer to a suitable container before placing in the fridge. The curry should not be eaten for 24 hours.

For variety you may like to add fresh herbs at the last five minutes of simmering. Coriander will work well as in the chicken curry.

Serve with a fresh green vegetables (snow peas, bok choy, etc.) and rice, for looks you can add saffron to the rice for yellow rice though cooking dies are cheaper, and for flavour you can cook the rice with dill or the coriander roots etc.

Coarse bread goes very well with this wet curry which should be medium to hot. If you would prefer the curry mild, use mild curry sauce. If you want the curry hotter, use more curry powder/spices, Tabasco or fresh chili, but this should also be added the day before and left for 24 hours.

chilli turkey

Serves 4

2 onions, finely chopped	200 g (7 oz) tinned organic navy beans, drained and washed
2 garlic cloves, crushed	
2 tablespoons olive oil	200 g (7 oz) tinned organic kidney beans
500 g (1 lb) turkey mince (ground turkey)	½ cup (4 fl oz) water
2 teaspoons of chilli powder	½ teaspoon sea salt
1 tablespoon Tabasco sauce	½ cup chopped fresh coriander (cilantro)
1 teaspoon cumin	1 red capsicum, diced
1 teaspoon pepper	400 g (14 oz) tin crushed tomatoes

In a large frying pan, sauté the onion and garlic in olive oil. Add the turkey and stir over medium heat for 10-15 minutes. Add the chilli, Tabasco, cumin and pepper and cook for a further 5 minutes.

Add the navy beans, water and sea salt and cook for a further 15 minutes. Add the coriander, capsicum and tomatoes and cook for a further 10-15 minutes. Serve over steamed vegetables or with a salad.

sesame lamb

2 medium onions, diced	1 cup (8 fl oz) red wine
1 carrot, diced	1 teaspoon mixed herbs
1 parsnip	3 bay leaves
2 teaspoons garlic, minced	8 mushrooms
cooking oil	fresh coriander to taste
3 bacon rashers	2 tablespoons sesame seeds
1 kg (2 lb) lamb leg meat	salt and pepper to taste

Heat diced onions, carrot, parsnip and garlic in oil. Add bacon and cook for a few minutes.

Added the lamb with red wine, mixed herbs, bay leaves, salt and pepper. Bring to boil (add a little water if necessary) then turn down to simmer for 30 minutes.

Add mushrooms, coriander leaves and sesame seeds and simmer a further 15 minutes.

Thicken as desired and serve.

Serve with a fresh green vegetables (snow peas, boc choy etc) and rice or potatoes, top off with a little fresh coriander.

Variety can be achieved by heating the dish with a small amount of hot chilli sauce, or by stirring in a tub of sour cream just before serving.

sweet treats

anzacs

Makes approximately 16 biscuits

125 g (4 oz) butter	100 g (3½ oz) rolled oats
1 tablespoon golden syrup	90 g (3 oz) desiccated (shredded) coconut
1 teaspoon bicarbonate of soda (see glossary)	125 g (4 oz) plain (all-purpose) flour
2 tablespoons boiling water	250 g (8 oz) raw sugar

Preheat oven to 155°C (315°F).

Melt butter and golden syrup in a large saucepan over a low heat.

In a cup, mix bicarbonate of soda and boiling water. Stir this through butter mixture.

In a bowl, combine dry ingredients and pour melted butter mixture into centre. Mix to a moist but firm consistency. Drop teaspoonfuls of mixture onto greased baking trays and press down flat.

Bake in the oven for 20 minutes, until golden brown. Leave biscuits on baking trays for a few minutes, then remove to a wire rack to completely cool.

apple crumble
with vanilla custard

Serves 8

6 Granny Smith apples, peeled, cored and sliced
3 cloves
½ cup (5 oz) honey
125 g (4 oz) plain wholemeal flour
100 g (3½ oz) oatmeal
30 g (1 oz) wheatgerm (see glossary)
¼ teaspoon salt
90 g (3 oz) raw sugar
185 g (6 oz) butter

VANILLA CUSTARD
1¼ cups (10 fl oz) milk
½ teaspoon vanilla essence
3 tablespoons caster (superfine) sugar
3 egg yolks

Preheat oven to 200°C (400°F).

Place apples in an ovenproof dish. Add cloves and pour over honey.

Place flour, oatmeal, wheatgerm, salt and sugar in a bowl. Rub in butter until mixture is crumbly, then spread mixture over apples.

Bake in the oven for one hour, or until top is golden brown. Serve with vanilla custard.

To make vanilla custard, heat milk in a saucepan over a low heat. Add vanilla essence and stir through. In a bowl, mix sugar and egg yolks until smooth. Add a little of the warmed milk to the egg mixture, stirring constantly, then add remaining milk. Return mixture to the saucepan, still on a low heat, and stir constantly, not allowing the mixture to boil, until it thickens and has the consistency of cream (it should coat the back of a metal spoon).

apple tart

Serves 6

PASTRY

180 g (6 oz) plain (all-purpose) flour
2 teaspoons baking powder (see glossary)
125 g (4 oz) butter
60 g (2 oz) rolled oats
2 tablespoons sugar
2 teaspoons lemon zest
1 egg yolk
egg white, beaten, for glazing

FILLING

1 x 400 g (13 oz) can pie apple
¾ cup (4 oz) sultanas
180 g (6 oz) brown sugar
1 teaspoon cinnamon
1 tablespoon lemon juice

TOPPING

30 g (1 oz) butter
2 tablespoons plain (all-purpose) flour
3 tablespoons brown sugar
30 g (1 oz) rolled oats

Preheat oven to 200°C (400°F).

To make pastry, sift flour and baking powder into a bowl. Rub in butter with your fingertips until mixture resembles fine breadcrumbs. Add rolled oats, sugar and lemon zest, then add egg yolk and water and make into a stiff dough.

To make filling, combine all filling ingredients in a bowl.

To make topping, combine dry ingredients in a bowl and rub butter through with your fingertips until the mixture resembles large crumbs.

Roll out pastry dough so that it will fit a large tart plate. Lay pastry in tart dish and brush with the beaten egg white. Pour apple filling in and sprinkle topping over.

Bake in the oven for 10 minutes, then reduce the temperature to 180°C (350°F) and cook for a further 40 minutes.

Serve with fresh cream.

banana cake

Serves 6–8

125 g (4 oz) butter
125 g (4 oz) caster (superfine) sugar
1 teaspoon vanilla
2 small eggs
3 small ripe bananas, mashed
250 g (8 oz) self-raising (self-rising) flour, sifted
1 teaspoon bicarbonate of soda (see glossary)
1 tablespoon milk
1 cup (8 fl oz) fresh cream, whipped

LEMON ICING
250 g (8 oz) icing (confectioners') sugar
4 tablespoons lemon juice

Preheat oven to 200°C (400°F).

In a bowl, cream butter, caster sugar and vanilla thoroughly. Add eggs, one at a time, beating well after each addition. Add bananas to mixture and combine well. Add half flour and fold in lightly.

Dissolve bicarbonate of soda in milk and add to mixture. Stir in gently. Add remaining flour and mix well.

Pour mixture into two greased and floured 20 cm (8 in) cake tins and bake in the oven for about 25 minutes. The cake is ready when a wooden skewer inserted into the centre comes out clean.

When cold, join cakes with cream and ice with lemon icing.

To make lemon icing, sift icing sugar into a bowl and add lemon juice. Stir until icing is smooth.

butter cake

Serves 6-8

125 g (4 oz) butter	180 g (6 oz) self-raising (self-rising) flour
100 g (3½ oz) caster (superfine) sugar	¾ teaspoon salt
½ teaspoon vanilla essence	3-4 tablespoons milk
2 eggs	

Preheat oven to 180°C (350°F).

Grease the inside of a 20 cm (8 in) spring-form cake tin and place a piece of greaseproof paper on the bottom.

Beat butter and sugar in a large bowl until light and creamy. Add vanilla essence and beat again. Beat eggs into the mixture, one at a time.

Sift flour and salt together. Add flour and milk alternately to egg mixture and beat gently until there are no lumps. Pour into cake tin and smooth the top. Bake cake on the centre shelf of the oven for 35 minutes. Leave cake to cool for a few minutes, then turn out onto a wire rack.

carrot cake

Serves 6–8

3 cups carrot, grated
2 cups (8 oz) plain (all-purpose) flour
2 cups (14 oz) caster (superfine) sugar
2 teaspoons baking soda (see glossary)
1 teaspoon baking powder (see glossary)
½ teaspoon salt
1 teaspoon ground cinnamon
4 eggs
1½ cups (12 fl oz) vegetable oil
1¼ teaspoons vanilla extract
1 x 225 g (8 oz) can crushed pineapple with juice
¾ cup (3 oz) pecans, chopped

CREAM CHEESE ICING

3½ cups (1 lb) icing (confectioners') sugar
1 x 250 g (8 oz) packet cream cheese
½ cup (4 oz) butter, softened
1¼ teaspoons vanilla extract
1 cup (4 oz) pecans, chopped, to garnish

Preheat oven to 175°C (350°F).

Grease and flour a 23 cm (9 in) spring-form cake tin. In a large bowl, combine carrots, flour, sugar, baking soda, baking powder, salt and cinnamon. Stir in eggs, oil, vanilla, pineapple and pecans. Spoon batter into prepared cake tin.

Bake for 30–40 minutes, or until a wooden skewer inserted into the centre of the cake comes out clean. Allow to cool.

To make cream cheese icing, combine icing sugar, cream cheese, butter and vanilla in a medium bowl. Beat mixture until smooth. Spread over cooled cake and sprinkle with pecans.

cheesecake

Serves 10

CRUST	FILLING
1 x 250 g (8 oz) packet plain sweet biscuits	250 g (8 oz) cream cheese
125 g (4 oz) butter	cup (2¾ fl oz) lemon juice
	1 x 395 g (13 oz) can sweetened condensed milk (see glossary)
	2 teaspoons nutmeg, grated

To make the crust, put biscuits in a plastic bag and seal the top with an elastic band or twist tie. Using a rolling pin, crush the biscuits in the bag – you will need to roll again and again until biscuits are finely crushed. Pour biscuit crumbs into a bowl.

Melt butter in a saucepan over medium heat, then pour over biscuit crumbs and mix thoroughly. Tip biscuit mixture into a 20 cm (8 in) spring-form cake tin and spread it out, then press it down firmly with the back of a spoon. Make sure you press some up the sides as well. The biscuit crust should be about 5 mm (¼ in) thick all over. Put the cake tin in the refrigerator for 20 minutes while you prepare the filling.

To make the filling, put the cream cheese in a bowl and mash it up with a fork. Add lemon juice and condensed milk and beat with an egg beater until the mixture is smooth. Pour cheese mixture into the cake tin and smooth over gently with a spoon. Sprinkle grated nutmeg on the top.

Put the cheesecake in the refrigerator and leave to set for at least four hours. You can garnish with sliced fruit or a dusting of icing sugar.

chocolate and date slice

Serves 6-8

1 cup (5 oz) dates, chopped	½ cup chocolate bits
125 g (4 oz) self-raising (self-rising) flour	125 g (4 oz) butter
250 g (8 oz) brown sugar	1 tablespoon golden syrup
45 g (1½ oz) desiccated (shredded) coconut	1 egg, beaten

Preheat oven to 180°C (350°F).

In a bowl, combine all the dry ingredients. In a small saucepan, melt butter and stir in golden syrup. Cool slightly then add egg and mix. Add melted butter mixture to the dry ingredients and mix together well.

Line a rectangular cake pan (about 30 x 20 cm/12 x 10 in) with baking paper (or just grease it) and pour mixture in. Press flat with the back of a spoon. Bake in the oven for 20-25 minutes, or until golden brown.

Variation: Add mixed fruit or mixed nuts instead of dates.

chocolate mousse

Serves 8

2 tablespoons brandy
5 eggs, separated

375 g (12 oz) good quality dark chocolate, chopped
1¼ cups (10 fl oz) thickened cream

In a small saucepan over low heat, beat brandy and egg yolks until smooth. Meanwhile, melt chocolate in a bowl over hot water, stirring until smooth. Cool chocolate, then whisk in the yolk mixture.

In another bowl, beat egg whites until they form soft peaks. In a third bowl, beat cream until stiff. Fold egg whites and cream into chocolate mixture until no streaks remain.

Spoon into eight mousse pots or one large serving dish. Cover and chill for at least three hours, or until set.

chocolate pudding

Serves 4

60 g (2 oz) self-raising (self-rising) flour
2 tablespoons cocoa
60 g (2 oz) breadcrumbs

60 g (2 oz) caster (superfine) sugar
1 egg
dash of milk
few drops vanilla essence

Sift flour and cocoa into a bowl, then add all other dry ingredients and mix thoroughly. In another bowl, beat egg and milk, then stir in vanilla essence.

Stir enough liquid into the dry mixture to give it a slightly sticky consistency. Grease and flour a bowl and put the mixture in it. Cover with greased greaseproof paper and steam or boil for about 1¾ hours.

Serve with vanilla custard.

chocolate walnut brownies

Makes 16 squares

60 g (2 oz) plain (all-purpose) flour
1 tablespoon bran
¼ teaspoon baking powder (see glossary)
60 g (2 oz) walnuts, chopped
60 g (2 oz) butter

60 g (2 oz) cooking chocolate
180 g (6 oz) brown sugar
2 eggs, beaten
½ teaspoon vanilla essence

Preheat oven to 180°C (350°F). Grease a 28 x 18 cm (11 x 7 in) shallow baking tin. Cut a piece of grease-proof paper large enough to line the tin, going a little higher than the edge of the tin. Press greaseproof paper inside the tin, cutting down into each corner so you can fold the paper round to fit.

In a bowl, mix together flour, bran, baking powder and walnuts.

In a saucepan, melt butter with chocolate and sugar. Cool slightly, then whisk in eggs and vanilla essence with a fork. Pour this into the flour mixture and mix well.

Pour mixture into the prepared tin and bake in the oven for 35 minutes, until the cake has risen and the centre springs back when lightly pressed. Leave to cool in the tin, then cut into squares.

lamingtons

Makes 12

1 x day-old standard butter cake, baked in 18 x 28 x 4 cm (7 x 11 x 1½ in) tin

CHOCOLATE COATING
750 g (1½ lb) caster (superfine) sugar
30 g (1 oz) cocoa
1 cup (8 fl oz) water
1 teaspoon vanilla essence
½–¾ cup (1-2 oz) desiccated (shredded) coconut (placed in a bowl)

Cut cake into 4 cm (1½ in) squares.

To make chocolate coating, put sugar, cocoa and water in a saucepan. Bring to the boil, stirring occasionally, then simmer for 12 minutes without stirring. Remove saucepan from heat, add vanilla and stir for one minute. Cool slightly. Stand mixture over hot water.

To coat lamingtons, spoon chocolate coating over to completely cover each square, then toss the squares in desiccated coconut. Place lamingtons on a wire rack so that coating can set.

lemon tart

Serves 8

CRUST	FILLING
400 g (13 oz) packet shortcrust pastry	4 eggs
icing (confectioners') sugar, to dust	2 egg yolks
	¼ cup (2 fl oz) lemon juice
	¼ cup (2 oz) sugar
	250 g (8 oz) sour cream

Preheat oven to 150°C (300°F).

Roll pastry out on a lightly floured surface to 4 mm (¼ in) thickness. Line a 20 cm (8 in) loose bottom flan tin with the pastry. Bake blind according to packet instructions. Cool pastry while preparing tart filling.

Lightly beat eggs, egg yolks, lemon juice, rind and sugar together until combined. Beat sour cream with a spoon to soften and stir into egg mixture until combined. Pour mixture through a sieve into the pastry shell.

Bake in the oven for 35–40 minutes or until filling has set. Cool. Remove tart from tin and serve dusted with icing sugar.

pavlova

Serves 8-12

3 egg whites
180 g (6 oz) caster (superfine) sugar
½ teaspoon cornflour (cornstarch)
½ teaspoon white vinegar
½ teaspoon vanilla essence

FILLING
1¼ cups (10 fl oz) cream
2-3 teaspoons icing (confectioners') sugar
½ teaspoon vanilla essence
250 g (8 oz) strawberries, washed and hulled
4 kiwifruit, peeled and sliced
6 passionfruit, pulp removed

Preheat oven to 120°C (250°F). In a bowl, whisk egg whites until they are quite stiff. Add sugar, a spoonful at a time, beating well to dissolve. Add cornflour with the last spoonful of sugar, then fold in vinegar and vanilla essence.

Draw an 18 cm (7 in) circle on greaseproof paper placed on a greased baking tray. Sprinkle lightly with cornflour. Spread the meringue mixture to cover the circle and shape into a cake, dome or pie shape — whatever you prefer. Place in the oven for 1½-2 hours, until crisp and dry. Open the oven door and cool before removing, then peel away the paper.

To make filling, whip cream in a bowl. Sweeten slightly with icing sugar and vanilla.

Serve pavlova with whipped cream piled on top and fruit arranged over fresh cream.

scones

Makes 12 scones

250 g (8 oz) plain (all-purpose) flour
2½ teaspoons baking powder (see glossary)
½ teaspoon salt

60 g (2 oz) butter
¾ cup (6 fl oz) milk

Preheat oven to 200°C (450°F).

Sift flour, baking powder and salt into a mixing bowl. Cut butter into flour in small pieces and rub in lightly with your fingertips until mixture resembles very fine breadcrumbs.

Make a well in the centre of the flour, pour in milk and mix to a soft dough. Turn dough onto a lightly floured board and knead very lightly until smooth. Roll out to 3 cm (1¼ in) thickness and cut into rounds using a cookie cutter.

Place rounds close together on a baking tray lined with baking paper and cook for 10–15 minutes, or until scones have risen and are golden. Serve warm with jam and whipped cream.

shortbread biscuits

Makes 16 biscuits

125 g (4 oz) butter	100 g (3½ oz) plain (all-purpose) flour
60 g (2 oz) caster (superfine) sugar	60 g (2 oz) rice flour
1 teaspoon vanilla essence	25 g (¾ oz) cornflour (cornstarch)

Preheat oven to 200°C (400°F) in a bowl, cream butter and sugar, then add vanilla. Slowly add flours and form a dough.

Place mixture onto a baking tray covered with baking paper. Place tray in the freezer for 10 minutes (or the refrigerator for 20 minutes). Roll out dough between two sheets of baking paper to a thickness of 7 mm (⅓ in). Cut into desired biscuit shape using cookie cutters.

Cook biscuits in the oven for about 10 minutes, or until golden brown.

rocky road

375 g (12 oz) block of plain milk chocolate
400 g (13oz) tin of condensed milk
250 g (8 oz) packet of marshmallows

250 g (8 oz) packet of glazed cherries, halved
200 g (6½ oz) packed salted peanuts

Melt the chocolate in a saucepan. Remove from heat for 1 minute and fold in condensed milk. Mix all the other ingredients in a bowl and pour the chocolate mixture over them. Mix gently and pour the mixture into a square tin. Allow to set in the refrigerator (normally ovenight). Cut into square pieces and serve with coffee or hot chocolate.

flourless orange and almond cake

Serves 8

250 g (8 oz) sugar
250 g (8 oz) almond meal
2 oranges, seedless

6 eggs
1 teaspoon baking powder

Pre-heat oven to moderate, 160°C (325°F).

Grease and flour a 25 cm (10 in) cake tin.

Wash oranges thoroughly then slice one into ½ cm (¼ in) thick wheels and line the bottom of the cake tin with it.

Prick the outside of the remaining orange with a fork, place in a microwave-proof container filled with water. Cook in the microwave or boil in a pot for 8 minutes or until very soft. Blend orange in a food processor to create a puree.

Whisk together sugar and eggs. Add almond meal and orange puree.

Place the mixture in the cake tin and bake for 30 minutes.

Serve with mint, date and orange salsa and chocolate mascarpone or just on its own.

biscotti di mandorla

baked almond bread
Makes 1 loaf

6 egg whites	200 g (6½ oz) whole almonds, peeled
50 g (2 oz) castor sugar	icing sugar
100 g (3½ oz) plain flour	

Whisk egg and add sugar till firm, fold in flour and almonds, place in non-stick bread tin and bake for 15 minutes at 180°C (350°F).

Allow to cool then slice thinly. Toast under a grill and serve with icing sugar.

cherry tart

Serves 8-10

PASTRY	FILLING
185 g (6 oz) plain flour	500 g (1 lb) cherries, pitted
½ teaspoon salt	185 g (6 oz) caster sugar
90 g (3 oz) butter	2 tablespoons redcurrant jelly
3 tablespoons water	

To make pastry, sift flour and salt into a bowl. Rub butter into flour with your fingertips until mixture resembles fine breadcrumbs. Add water gradually and mix, with a round-bladed knife, to firm dough. Knead lightly. Cover with clingwrap, and chill in the refrigerator for 30 minutes.

Preheat oven to 220°C (420°F). Roll out pastry to a thickness of 5 mm (¼ in), and line a 20 cm (8 in) pie dish. Trim excess pastry from the edge of the pie dish. Pour cherries into the pie dish and sprinkle caster sugar over. Bake in the oven for 25 minutes. About 5 minutes before tart is ready, spread redcurrant jelly over the cherries, then return tart to the oven for the final 5 minutes.

Allow tart to cool, then chill and serve cold.

date slice

Makes 24 squares

125 g (4 oz) self-raising flour	150 g (5 oz) dates, chopped
60 g (2 oz) desiccated coconut	125 g (4 oz) butter
60 g (2 oz) caster sugar	lemon icing

Preheat oven to 180°C (350°F). Sift flour into a bowl and mix in coconut, sugar and dates. Melt butter in a saucepan over a low heat. Add melted butter to dry mixture and mix thoroughly with a wooden spoon.

Put mixture into a greased slice tin and press down firmly with the back of a spoon. Place slice on the centre shelf of the oven and bake for 25 minutes.

Remove slice from oven and cover with lemon icing while it is still hot. Cut into squares while it is still warm, but leave it in the tin to cool.

lime and ginger tart

Serves 8-10

PASTRY	CUSTARD
100 g (3½ oz) caster sugar	9 eggs
200 g (7 oz) unsalted butter	300 g (11 oz) caster sugar
1 egg	300 ml (10 fl oz) cream
300 g (11 oz) plain flour	350 ml (11½ fl oz) strained lime juice
	1 tablespoon finely chopped lime zest
	30 g (1 oz) finely chopped crystallised ginger

To make the pastry, preheat oven to 180°C (350°F). Cream sugar and butter until light and fluffy. Add egg and mix briefly. Add flour and combine. Turn pastry onto a lightly floured bench and knead lightly. Rest in refrigerator for 1 hour. Roll out to fit a 25 cm (10 in) flan tin with removable base.

Line pastry with foil, fill with uncooked rice, lentils or beans. Place in oven and bake blind for 20 minutes. Remove foil and rice and return to oven for another 15 minutes. The pastry should be crisp and pale gold.

To make the custard, preheat oven to 160°C (300°F). Whisk the eggs and sugar in a bowl until combined. Stir in all the other ingredients. Carefully pour custard mix in tart shell and take for 40 minutes.

The tart should still be a little wobbly in the centre. Remove from oven and cool on cake rack to allow the custard to finish setting. Serve at room temperature.

A variation on the classic lemon tart. Looks deceptively simple, but requires some technical skills to perfect.

glazed apple flan

Serves 8

1 batch olive oil pastry	1 teaspoon nutmeg, grated
1 egg white	2 tablespoons no-cane-sugar raspberry preserve
2 green apples	1 tablespoon water
1 orange zest, finely grated and juice of half orange	

Use ¾ of this amount of pastry for a 24 cm (9½ in) diameter x 2 cm (¾ in) deep loose-based tart or quiche tin. Roll the pastry out between two pieces of cling wrap to about ½ cm thick and line the tart/quiche tin. Trim and put in the freezer for 25 minutes. Remove and refrigerate for 10 minutes.

Preheat oven to 200°C (350°F). Take the raw pastry case from the refrigerator, prick using fork and bake for 10 minutes. Lift from the oven and brush with some lightly beaten egg white. Let sit for a few minutes while you prepare the apples.

Core and halve the apples, from stem to base. Cut into half-moon slices making sure the apple half stays in place and the apple slices sit tightly together. Place in bowl and sprinkle over the orange zest and orange juice. Let sit for 2 minutes then fan the drained, sliced apples around the partially cooked pastry base. Do this in a circular movement starting with the outside first and working in the centre. Flatten the sliced apple halves as you fan them. Make sure the apples are well drained and all the zest is on top of the sliced apples.

Cook in the oven for 35–40 minutes or until the apples are breaking down.

Remove and cool for 3 minutes then sprinkle with the nutmeg. Melt the preserve and water in microwave for 30 seconds, brush over the top of the apples and put back into the oven for 10 minutes. Lift from the oven and cool before removing the base and slicing. Serve with low-fat vanilla ice-cream.

measurements

OVEN TEMPERATURES

100°C	very slow	200°F	Gas Mark 1
120°C	very slow	250°F	Gas Mark 1
150°C	slow	300°F	Gas Mark 2
165°C	warm	325°F	Gas Mark 2-3
180°C	moderate	350°F	Gas Mark 4
190°C	moderately hot	375°F	Gas Mark 5
200°C	moderately hot	400°F	Gas Mark 6
220°C	hot	420°F	Gas Mark 7
230°C	very hot	450°F	Gas Mark 8
250°C	very hot	485°F	Gas Mark 9

FLUID MEASURES

Metric	Imperial	Standard Cups
30 ml	1 fl oz	2 tablespoons
60 ml	2 fl oz	¼ cup
80 ml	2¾ fl oz	⅓ cup
125 ml	4 fl oz	½ cup
250 ml	8 fl oz	1 cup
500 ml	16 fl oz	2 cups
750 ml	24 fl oz	3 cups
1 L	32 fl oz	4 cups

SOLID MEASURES

Metric	Imperial
10 g	⅓ oz
15 g	½ oz
20 g	⅔ oz
30 g	1 oz
45 g	1½ oz
60 g	2 oz
100 g	3½ oz
125 g	4 oz
150 g	5 oz
165 g	5½ oz
180 g	6 oz
200 g	6½ oz
250 g	8 oz
300 g	10 oz
350 g	11½ oz
400 g	13 oz
500 g	1 lb
750 g	1½ lb
1 kg	2 lb

glossary

Almond meal: Skinless, blanched almonds that have been finely ground. Almond meal gives a moist texture and rich, buttery flavour to cakes, cookies, muffins and sweet breads. It is low in carbohydrates and a good source of protein, fibre, vitamin E and magnesium.

Allspice: The dried berry of the pimiento tree. The dried berries are dark brown and are available whole or ground. The whole berries are used in pickles, preserves and chutney and when ground as a flavouring in cakes, soups and meat dishes.

Baking powder: A leavener containing a mixture of baking soda and cornstarch. When mixed with liquid it releases carbon dioxide gas bubbles that cause a bread or cake to rise.

Baking soda: see Bicarbonate of soda.

Bicarbonate of soda: Also known as baking soda, this is used as a leavener in baked foods.

Champignons: A young closed mushroom with a subtle flavour ideal for marinades, risottos and salads.

Dill pickles: Pickles preserved in seasoned brine or vinegar and dill.

Dry mustard: Finely ground mustard seeds, also referred to as powdered mustard. Used to flavour meats and vegetables or as an ingredient in salad dressings.

Glucose syrup: A mixture of sugars derived from starch. Used as a sweetener in drinks and desserts.

Grapeseed oil: An oil extracted from grape seeds, which is commonly used in salad dressings.

Mace: The red membrane that surrounds nutmeg. It is a pungent spice used in chutneys, pickles and sauces.

Marsala: A rich, smoky-flavoured fortified wine from Sicily. Flavour ranges from sweet to dry.

Milk, scalded: Milk heated to almost boiling point so that small bubbles form around the edge of the pan and a film appears over the surface of the liquid.

Saffron: The dried stigmas of the crocus flower. Gold in colour, it is an aromatic spice with a pungent, slightly bitter flavour. Used in paella and bouillabaise.

Seasoned flour: Plain flour with a pinch of salt and pepper mixed through. Mixed herbs can also be added for a more intense flavour.

Sunflower seed meal: De-hulled sunflower seeds that have been finely ground. They are a good source of protein and fibre.

Sweetened condensed milk: Evaporated milk that has had its water content reduced, and has been sweetened and thickened with sugar.

Tarragon vinegar: Vinegar steeped with the herb tarragon.

Truss: To secure meat or poultry with string or skewers so that the food maintains its shape during cooking.

Vermicelli: Very fine strands of spaghetti.

Wheat, cracked: Whole wheat grains broken into coarse, medium or fine fragments. Available from health food stores.

Wheatgerm: The embryo of a wheat grain. A source of vitamins, minerals and protein. It has a nutty flavour and is very oily. Available from health food stores.

index

First published in Australia in 2005 by
New Holland Publishers (Australia) Pty Ltd
Sydney • Auckland • London • Cape Town

1/66 Gibbes Street Chatswood NSW 2067 Australia
218 Lake Road Northcote Auckland New Zealand
86 Edgware Road London W2 2EA United Kingdom
80 McKenzie Street Cape Town 8001 South Africa

Updated edition published in 2009.

10 9 8 7 6 5 4 3 2 1

A record of this book is available from the National Library of Australia.

ISBN 9781741108576

Publisher: Fiona Schultz
Publishing Manager: Lliane Clarke
Editors: Monica Berton, Ashlea Wallington
Designer: Joanne Buckley, Tania Gomes
Photographer: Joe Filshie
Production Manager: Olga Dementiev
Printer: SNP/ Leefung Printing Co. Ltd (China)

The publisher gratefully acknowledges the following authors for their contribution of recipes from these New Holland titles:

Blue Eye Dragon; Muriel Chen, pp 168
Delicious Living; Peter Howard, pp 18, 19, 43, 47, 48, 98, 153, 194, 229
Diabetes Eat and Enjoy; Christine Roberts, Jennifer McDonald and Margaret Cox, pp 100
Eat, Taste, Nourish; Zoe Bingley-Pullin, 42, 50, 57, 58, 131, 132, 170, 197, 200
Essentially Japanese; Hideo Dekura, pp 21
Frostbite; Susan Austin, pp 37, 38, 39, 40, 41, 49, 51, 54, 55, 99, 195, 196
Live & Cookin' @ Lizottes; Brian Lizotte, pp 101, 102, 224
Make it Moroccan; Hassan M'Souli, pp 22, 23
Now Vegan; Lynda Stoner, pp 90, 107, 108, 130
Ristorante Fellini; Tony Purcuoco; pp 103, 104, 105, 106, 129, 225
Spirit House; Helen Brierty and Annette Fear; pp 172, 173, 228
The Basic Cookbook; Lesley Pagett and Yvette Thompson; pp 36, 46, 59, 60, 109, 126, 148, 149, 152, 171, 226, 227
The Press Club; George Calombaris, pp 128